The Anglo-American Loan of 1946:
U.S. Economic Opportunism and the Start of the Cold War

By
Darden Callaway

A Thesis Submitted to the Davidson College Department of History
Kendrick K. Kelley Program

April 7, 2014
Davidson, North Carolina

Contents:

## Acknowledgements

This project would not have been possible without the constant support and guidance of the Davidson College History Department. In particular, Dr. Jane Mangan and Dr. Dan Aldridge's detailed advice and careful readings of my draft were invaluable. Dr. Mangan has helped me wrestle with complex ideas (and emotions), while also helping me perfect my writing. As my second reader, Dr. Aldridge patiently explained complex political developments in American history. I also want to thank Dr. Vivien Dietz and Dr. Mangan for their support in the beginning stages of the project, even volunteering to be my "cheerleaders" throughout the year. Dr. Andrew Fiss offered to serve as my third reader, for which I am extremely grateful. I am honored to have participated in this program and would never have realized my full potential as a historian without such dedicated professors.

Beyond Davidson, special recognition is due to the archives at Cambridge University and the London School of Economics. Gemma Ward at Churchill College and Peter Monteith at King's College were both essential in the planning and execution of my abroad research. Dr. William Leuchtenburg at the University of North Carolina Chapel Hill welcomed me to his home for a rewarding brainstorming session in September, lent me numerous books and sources, and was a constant source of advice throughout the experience. After helping my father on his senior thesis in 1984, Dr. Leuchtenburg brought the same enthusiasm to my project. His expertise was inspiring and invaluable.

The Kelley Program has been a defining experience for me. I am forever grateful to my fellow Kelley scholars, especially Chelsea Creta, for their critical advice, moral support, and humor. My trip to London, Oxford, and Cambridge challenged me to take my work to new levels. My parents and roommates let me bounce ideas off of them and learned far more about the 1946 loan than they had ever anticipated – whether they liked it or not. Anne Tabb, a 2013 graduate of Davidson and of the Kelley Program, offered unparalleled moral support and advice. The John Montgomery Belk Scholarship at Davidson has provided me with a safety net and with the motivation to continuously go above and beyond what is expected of me. I especially want to thank the family of Kendrick K. Kelley for giving this opportunity to now twenty-six years of Davidson students.

Lastly, I dedicate this project to the late Professor Godfrey LeMay of Worcester College, University of Oxford, who provided me with incredible inspiration and introduced me to the particular complexities of modern Anglo-American relations.

## Preface

The Anglo-American Loan of 1946 marked a turning point in world history: the start of the American-dominated post-war economic order. The loan coincided with Britain's economic turmoil, the beginnings of the demise of the British Empire, increasing controversies over socialism and communism, and America's acceptance of economic interventionism. It is a microcosm of larger changes in the post-war world order. This loan shows the fluidity of the events surrounding the end of World War II and the Cold War. It was both cause and consequence of the Cold War and Britain's economic subordination. Thus, the governing question for this paper is to determine the loan's role in the United States' assertion of global economic dominance in the postwar world.

During the mid-nineteenth century, the United Kingdom was the birthplace of the industrial revolution. Its empire was vast and prosperous. Later in that century, rival industrial powerhouses developed in Germany and the United States. The First World War and the depression of the 1930s disproportionately hurt England and Germany, as opposed to the United States. However, they remained very important in the world economy. The Second World War exhausted the economies and industrial capacity of both countries. After combat ended, the shortages, hunger and misery continued. Surprising the British victors, the economic sacrifices of wartime did not give way to prosperity.

Meanwhile, the United States, relieved that the war was over, was ready to withdraw from international affairs and focus internally. President Truman abruptly ended Lend-Lease, which had been a financial lifeline for Britain. Britain was forced to beg for money from America, which, after heated debate, resulted in the Anglo-American Loan of 1946. This agreement provided desperately needed financial assistance to postwar Britain between the periods of the Lend-Lease program and the Marshall Plan. The loan was a pivotal event in defining the post-war relationship of Britain and the United States and signaled the economic ascendancy of America.

Did the United States help or hurt Britain with this loan? Was the United States acting as a friendly benefactor or as an opportunistic competitor? The answers are mixed. The loan was absolutely necessary to a desperate Britain, and the United States undoubtedly saved Britain from default. Still, the stipulations placed on the loan were favorable to the American economic system. American politicians took advantage of Britain's financial despair to impose loan requirements that would serve its multilateral trade agenda. The immense sacrifices of the British during World War II had sentimental value, but had no currency in the new economic system. The American approach to the loan was an example of the return to power politics after the war. Instead, Britain was forced to accept its own declining economic and political power, unwillingly subscribing to the rising American agenda.

This paper will examine the loan and its consequences. First, it will consider the economic and political context of the loan. Next, it will examine the Keynes-Halifax mission and the drafting of the loan, detailing how a $5 billion grant proposal became a $3.75 billion loan with substantial conditions. The third chapter will discuss British reluctance to accept the conditions of the loan. The following chapter will show how the hesitant Americans were convinced to finance British recovery through the loan. The final chapter will demonstrate the profound near-term consequences of the loan, analyzing the dramatic shift it caused in international relations.

In the years immediately following the act's passage, most scholars participate in the debate surrounding the loan rather than offering impartial commentary. For example, Roy

Harrod, an English economist and member of the Liberal Party, published a biography of John

Maynard Keynes in 1951, just six years after the loan had been enacted.[1] Harrod was well known

for his economic growth model and political advocacy of Keynesian public spending and the

removal of import barriers. Harrod also wrote a critique of prominent Conservative politician

Leopold Amery's *The Washington Loan Agreements: A Critical Study of American Foreign*

*Policy* in 1947.[2] Because of this lack of temporal perspective, contemporary documents such as

these from the years following the loan are less useful as secondary sources. Harrod's goal is not

to unbiasedly place the loan in the larger context of history, but rather to further his own political

agenda. Those contemporary scholars who did not wish to espouse a political opinion focused

narrowly on the on the loan documents themselves. Alex Rosenson offers an in-depth analysis of

the financial terms of the agreement rather than considering the loan's repercussions, thus

limiting his analysis of the loan's role in a larger, global context.[3]

In more recent years, most historians have considered the loan as evidence of England's

decline, rather than as a direct stimulus of the new world order and Britain's acceptance of

American economic values. Little attention is paid to the role of the loan in cementing the

dollar's status as the dominant international currency or in the implementation of the Bretton

Woods institutions (the World Bank and the International Monetary Fund). In addition, it is often

argued that the loan was passed because of mounting Soviet-American tensions, but its role in

---

[1] Roy F. Harrod, *The Life of John Maynard Keynes* (London: Macmillan, 1951). Harrod was an English economist, well known for his economic growth model and his biography of John Maynard Keynes. It is thought that he would have been awarded the Nobel Prize had he lived longer. He was a member of the Liberal party, and strongly advocated the elimination of import barriers and Keynesian public spending. See also: *The Life of John Maynard Keynes* (London: Macmillan, 1951), "The Harrod-Damar Growth Model" (1964), and Ing. Marta Martincová's profile of "Roy Forbes Harrod," Národná banka Slovenska, http://www.nbs.sk/_img/Documents/BIATEC/BIA12_02/25_28.pdf.

[2] Amery was one of the most vocal British critics of the loan. Roy F. Harrod. "Review of *The Washington Loan Agreements: A Critical Study of American Foreign Policy* by L.S. Amery," *International Affairs* 23, no. 1 (January 1947).

[3] Alex Rosenson, "The Terms of the Anglo-American Financial Agreement," *The American Economic Review* 37, no. 1 (March 1947): 178–187. http://www.jstor.org/stable/1802868.

exacerbating Cold War tensions is never considered. The loan required American politicians to directly compare the merits of a Soviet-American alliance and an Anglo-American alliance. Because both countries requested a loan at the same time, negotiators like William Clayton in the State Department were forced to prioritize. The loan deserves much more credit for its reorganization of the political and economic order after the war than it currently receives. The loan is a key signifier of the new Cold War era that many historians ignore.[4]

Those who do address the loan in depth tend to be nationally self-absorbed, describing only its impact on their own country. American historian Lloyd C. Gardner uses Will Clayton, the U.S. negotiator of the loan, as an example of how "the United States was more responsible for the *way* in which the Cold War developed" than usually assumed.[5] As a result, Gardner's focus is on American politicians' considerations of the loan, especially in the regards to Soviet-American relations. He argues that without the loan, the United States would have been unable to pursue an economic agenda of multilateralism that was opposed to Soviet interests. The loan's real role, for Gardner, was its position "at the heart of American determination to restore a completely open world, and…it[s] suggest[ion of] what could be done with economic power. In that sense, it was a turning point."[6] He ignores the British perspective of the loan, portraying them instead as passive beneficiaries.

Likewise, Bert Cochran's documentation of the Truman presidency mentions the loan in passing, asserting that it, along with the Truman Doctrine, changed American attitudes toward Europe. The loan's failure to relieve England convinced Americans that Europe would not immediately recover from the financial burdens of war.[7] Free trade was an essential tool for

---

[4] In September 1947, the Soviet Union created the coniform, whose goal was to strengthen the communist political influence in the Eastern bloc and expand it towards other countries.

[5] Gardner refutes scholars who blame the Soviet Union's broken promises at Yalta and expansionism for the Cold War. Lloyd C. Gardner, *Architects of Illusion*, (Chicago: Quadrangle Books, 1970), x.

[6] Gardner, *Architects*, 118.

promoting international peace, as exhibited by the loan's stipulations. Gabriel Kolko criticizes this American effort to impose capitalism on the rest of the world, calling it the "key to the problem of the politics and diplomacy of World War II."[8] Both Kolko and Cochran ignore the British mistrust of the United States that arose as a result of the loan, and like Gardner, assume that the loan marked a shift in the United States' views of its allies, not England and the Soviet Union's views of the United States. The British remain passive recipients in Cochran's description.

British historians have the same biased lens, surveying only England's view of the loan. Peter Clarke's *The Last Thousand Days of the British Empire* uses the loan to show how Britain emerged from the war only to discover that they would not be rewarded for their sacrifices. He disregards both the American trepidations regarding the loan as well as its economic implications, focusing only on its moral effect on Great Britain.[9] Unlike these one-sided documentations, this paper will provide a bilateral analysis, transcending nationalist history by including both British and American positions on the loan.

Scholars also often simplify the debates in Parliament and Congress by assuming they were drawn along party lines, with clear arguments defining each side. Robin Edmonds is one culprit of this oversimplification. In the United States, he argues that prominent Republican Arthur Vandenberg's support and Soviet tensions allowed for the passage. He assumes that the British parties uniformly objected to the loan because of domestic concerns on the left and imperial fears on the right, but that economic despair mandated an approval.[10] Instead of

---

[7] Bert Cochran, *Harry Truman and the Crisis Presidency* (New York: Funk & Wagnalls, 1973), 192.

[8] Gabriel Kolko, *The Politics of War: The World and United States Foreign Policy, 1943-1945* (New York: Random House, 1968), 7.

[9] Peter Clarke, *The Last Thousand Days of the British Empire: Churchill, Roosevelt, and the Birth of the Pax Americana* (New York: Bloomsbury Press, 2009), 343.

[10] Robin Edmonds, *Setting the Mould: The United States and Britain 1945-1950*, (New York and London: W.W. Norton and Company, 1986), 102.

examining the complex political debates in each country, Edmonds relies on simplified stereotypes. This typecasting ignores the unexpected political alliances that formed during the debates. His conclusion is simply that "British pride and the American prejudice…combined to produce the terms of the Financial Agreement of 1945."[11] The reality was much more complicated, and a closer examination of the political debates is essential.

Other authors consider the loan only in an economic context. In Catherine Schenk's economic history of sterling's decline, she calls the Anglo-American loan of 1946 a "negotiat[ion] of sterling's decline as reserve currency."[12] Schenk argues that sterling convertibility, one condition of the loan, revealed the international community's doubt as to whether sterling (and the British Empire) as a solid investment. She also focuses on the loan's role in ensuring the development of Bretton Woods's international institutions. Schenk ignores the politics of the loan, instead documenting the financial aspects of the negotiations and of the loan's repercussions. She presents the negotiators as pure economists, devoid of any political motivations.

Similarly, Charles Kindleberger's first-of-its-kind history of Western European finance discusses the British loan as the key to Bretton Woods. Without sterling's participation, Bretton Woods may not have come into existence. Kindleberger includes no discussion of the loan negotiations, saying only that they were "laborious," and instead focuses on the loan's long-term consequences.[13] Fred Block also focuses on Bretton Woods and the loan's role in evaluating the popularity of imposing multilateralism on the rest of the world. He idealizes the American "struggle…to restore an open world economy after World War II" and works to highlight that in

---

[11] Edmonds, 105.

[12] Catherine R. Schenk, *The Decline of Sterling: Managing the Retreat of an International Currency, 1945-1992* (Cambridge, U.K.: Cambridge University Press, 2010), 31.

[13] Charles P. Kindleberger, *A Financial History of Western Europe* (New York and Oxford, U.K.: Oxford University Press, 1993), 419.

the early stages of the Cold War, this struggle was actually against European national capitalism, not Soviet communism.[14] Block includes the American political factions that debated the loan, but only in terms of whether they advocated that the country take an interventionist role or laissez-faire attitude in world economic affairs.

Those few historians who do attempt to bridge both American and British perspectives and economic and political consequences of the loan fail to consider the entire period the loan affected (from negotiations to afterlife). Robert Hathaway seeks to dismantle the assumption that any international interaction aside from Soviet-American was insignificant during the Cold War, arguing that the Anglo-American relationship also added to the tensions.[15] Britain was not simply the recipient of American policies. The fierce loan negotiations and reactions in the British press prove that England did not easily accept the American economic agenda. However, Hathaway only focuses on the loan's negotiations rather than on the debates following. In doing so, Hathaway ignores the political nature of American motives and British fears surrounding the agreement. He also disregards the long-term implications of the loan, both politically and economically. Ritchie Ovendale also focuses on the importance of the Anglo-American alliance in the Cold War, briefly mentioning the loan as part of the "inheritance" British politicians received upon the outset of the Soviet tensions.[16] Ovendale argues that the loan is another example of Americans' initial reluctance to form an Anglo-American alliance against the Soviet Union. Meanwhile, Ernest Bevin, Winston Churchill, and their colleagues emphasized the Anglo-American alliance as a key weapon to fighting the Cold War.

---

[14] Fred Block, *The Origins of International Economic Disorder: A Study of United States International Monetary Policy From World War II to the Present*, (Berkeley, Los Angeles, and London: University of California Press, 1977), 10.

[15] Robert Hathaway, *Ambiguous Partnership: Britain and America, 1944-1947.* (New York: Columbia University Press, 1981).

[16] Ritchie Ovendale, *The English-Speaking Alliance: Britain, the United States, the Dominions and the Cold War 1945-1951* (London: George Allen & Unwin Ltd., 1985), 3-4.

The most complete analysis of the 1946 Anglo-American loan is Richard N. Gardner's *Sterling-Dollar Diplomacy*.[17] Gardner's history of "international economic diplomacy," uses the loan as an example of the dichotomy between political jargon and economic policies at the end of World War II. American and British economists needed to "couch their statesmen's declaration [of partnership] in more concrete terms that may serve as a basis for actual negotiation of a draft agreement."[18] Gardner successfully combines the political and economic aspects of the loan negotiations, debates, and consequences. He argues that the loan failed to achieve the American goal of multilateralism and outlines three failures of American post-war economic policy: the idea that economic policies can achieve peace, the goal of uniform policies towards every country, and the attachment to formal agreements rather than "informal working relationships" to promote international collaboration.[19] Gardner is pessimistic about the future of multilateralism, and he sees the loan as one instance of American idealism's failure to align with the post-war reality. He argues that the requirements of convertibility and nondiscrimination were against British interests, ignoring the fact that both were actually goals of many British politicians in order to restore sterling's international reputation.

This paper bridges these gaps and develops a comprehensive understanding of the loan and its effects. It is an international history, including both the American and British perspectives. It also considers both the economic and political consequences of the loan. In particular, it takes a more detailed look at the political debates surrounding the loan, offering a more nuanced interpretation of each country's concerns at the end of the war.

---

[17] Robert Trifflin, Forward to Richard N. Gardner, *Sterling Dollar Diplomacy: The Origins and the Prospects of Our International Economic Order* (New York: McGraw-Hill Book Company, 1969).

[18] Robert Trifflin, Forward to Gardner, *Sterling Dollar Diplomacy*, xiv.

[19] Gardner, *Sterling Dollar Diplomacy*, 384.

This paper also draws connections between the different transitions the loan influenced, including the end of World War II, the move from the British Empire to American imperialism, the development of international economic institutions, the beginning of the Cold War, and the transition from Lend-Lease to the Marshall Plan. Without considering the loan in each of these contexts, past scholars have failed to realize the loan's role in the development of the post-war order. While it is often difficult to determine the loan's exact role in many of these developments, a thorough examination of the negotiation, debates, and consequences of the loan will reveal how it transformed the Anglo-American partnership. This offers insight into how American politicians were able to manipulate the post-war situation to their commercial and political advantage, forcing Britain to accept an American-mandated trade system.

<u>Chapter One: The Transition to Peace</u>

The Anglo-American relationship emerged when Britain and the United States fought as allies in the First World War. During the 1930s, Prime Minster Neville Chamberlain worked to gain the support of a reluctant, isolationist, and economically depressed United States for Britain against the increasingly aggressive Nazi regime.[20] The military alliance was once again formalized under Prime Minister Churchill and U.S. President Franklin Roosevelt with the signing of Lend-Lease in March 1941, and the American declaration of war in December of that year. By 1945, the Anglo-American partnership had become so strong that Allied Supreme Commander and future U.S. President Dwight Eisenhower announced in his first major speech, "even as I proclaim my undying Americanism, I am bold enough and exceedingly proud to claim basic kinship to you of London."[21] The two countries were emotionally bound by their shared wartime experiences.

As a result, what began as a military alliance had, by the end of the war, apparently become a deeply ingrained cooperation between American and British leaders that would largely determine the post-war world order. At his 1946 speech at Fulton, Missouri, ex-Prime Minister Churchill argued that a strong "fraternal association of the English speaking peoples" would develop a balance of power essential to combating Soviet influence and dismantling the "iron curtain."[22] What Churchill labeled "the special relationship" had transformed from a military coalition to the idea of "almost a single state."[23] This high-flown rhetoric does not reflect the

---

[20] Ovendale, 3-4.
[21] Dwight D. Eisenhower, "Guildhall Address," (Speech, London, June 12, 1945), http://www.eisenhower.archives.gov/education/bsa/citizenship_merit_badge/speeches_national_historical_importan ce/guildhall_address.pdf.
[22] Winston S. Churchill, "The Sinews of Peace" (Speech, Fulton, Missouri, Westminster College, March 5, 1946), http://www.winstonchurchill.org/learn/speeches/speeches-of-winston-churchill/120-the-sinews-of-peace. John W. Young, *Winston Churchill's Last Campaign: Britain and the Cold War 1951-1955*. (Oxford: Clarendon Press, 1996), 29.
[23] John W. Young, *Winston Churchill's Last Campaign: Britain and the Cold War, 1951-1955* (Oxford:

reality of the Anglo-American relationship during the war, which also had many areas of conflict, but reveals Churchill's faith in the partnership as a solution to the post-war power vacuum. No longer a marriage of convenience, the collaboration had infiltrated all aspects of each nation's operations. Although there were still areas of tension, the alliance had become a foundational block of international security, especially as Soviet-Western relations cooled.

In particular, British officials like Churchill anticipated the need to shift from a military to an economic alliance with the United States. The American wartime Lend-Lease program had become a constant flow of support upon which the country had come to depend, offering Britain over $31 billion in supplies.[24] Because the arrangement was considered a military strategy, American politicians never expected the loan to be fully paid back. When Roosevelt first introduced the idea of Lend-Lease to Congress, he argued for "leaving out the dollar mark in the form of a dollar debt and substitute it for a gentleman's obligation to repay in kind."[25] In 1943, Lord Halifax, the British ambassador to the United States, set the stage for continued financial support of Britain during a speech at Purdue University, saying, "You and I should think little of a man of great riches who had no sense of responsibility to his community and was purely self-indulgent and thought only of amusing himself. The same law goes for great nations."[26] Halifax's statement outlines Britain's assumption that the U.S. would help finance post-war reconstruction. At the Second Quebec Conference in September 1944, Churchill requested, and Roosevelt promised, $6 billion in post-war lend-lease aid from the U.S. to Britain.[27] British

---

Clarendon Press, 1996), 21. Young is the Chair of International History at the University of Nottingham. For more by the author, see *Britain, France, The Unity of Europe, 1945-1951* (Leicester University Press, 1984) and *International Relations Since 1945: A Global History* (Oxford: Oxford University Press, 2003).

[24] "Supplying the Allies: The U.S. Lend-Lease Program," *World War II Behind Closed Doors*, PBS, http://www.pbs.org/behindcloseddoors/in-depth/supplying-allies.html.

[25] Franklin D. Roosevelt, "On Lend Lease," (Press Conference, Washington, D.C., December 14, 1940) http://docs.fdrlibrary.marist.edu/odllpc2.html.

[26] Lord Halifax, "An English Gentleman Speaks to Americans," (Speech, West Lafayette, IN, Purdue University, June 21, 1943), Indiana State Library.

[27] United States Department of State, *Foreign Relations of the United States: Diplomatic Papers, 1944*

11

politicians planned for continued American financial support to smooth the transition from war to peace, since there was no reason for them to consider the alternative.

England's financial concerns were the primary motivation for continued Anglo-American partnership, but Parliamentarians also had other reasons to support the alliance. Ex-Prime Minister Churchill and the new Labour Foreign Secretary, Ernest Bevin, placed special emphasis on the relationship as a way to keep Britain politically relevant at the onset of the Cold War. Churchill's faith in Anglo-American collaboration was due to his belief "in the balance of power relationships rather than ideological conflict."[28] He recognized that the alliance would protect Britain from being internationally isolated and from anti-democratic influences. Clement Attlee, the Labour leader who won the Prime Minister's office in 1945, was an idealist committed to "international socialism" and the role of global organizations like the United Nations as facilitators of peace.[29] Attlee's Labour party proposed that international cooperation was necessary to "build a new United Nations, allies in a new war on hunger, ignorance, and want."[30] He valued the Anglo-American relationship as a vital weapon for international government and peacekeeping, as well as a way to keep his new administration's goals economically viable.

For Americans, continuing to support Britain was not a top priority, since their own economic prospects were not as rosy as the British imagined. Ending war contracts meant a huge drop in government spending, which fell from $84 billion in 1945 to less than $30 billion in 1946.[31] In one year, real GDP fell 10.9%, only beginning to rise only in the spring of 1947.[32]

---

(Washington, D.C.: Government Printing Office, 1944): 169. Referenced at http://images.library.wisc.edu/FRUS/EFacs/1944/reference/frus.frus1944.i0010.pdf. See also: John L. Chase, "The Development of the Morgenthau Plan Through the Quebec Conference," *The Journal of Politics* 16, no. 2 (May 1954): 324–59.

[28] John W. Young, *Winston Churchill's Last Campaign: Britain and the Cold War, 1951-1955* (Oxford: Clarendon Press, 1996), 29.

[29] Kenneth Harris, *Attlee* (New York and London: W.W. Norton & Company, 1982), 294.

[30] National Executive Committee of the Labour Party, "Let U.S. Face the Future: A Declaration of Labour Policy for the Consideration of the Nation," (April 1945): 11.

[31] Jason E. Taylor and Richard K. Vedder, "Stimulus by Spending Cuts: Lessons from 1946," *Cato Policy*

Over 10 million people were released from the armed services, and many wondered how the country would cope with the influx of workers and de-stimulus. In addition, most industries were benefitted from the increased demand of the war effort. Historian Jack Ballard called this rapid military and economic demobilization "the shock of peace."[33] Despite these drawbacks, the United States had undoubtedly emerged from the war stronger than Britain had. American's fear of postwar economic collapse outweighed the reality of their transition. Unemployment rates rose, but stayed below 4.5 percent between 1945 and 1948. Civilian employment actually expanded by four million jobs in the first two years, since pent up consumer demand compensated for the lack of government spending.[34] Higher standards of living and the baby boom meant more customers, and the growth of the automobile industry meant more jobs. Depression was largely avoided, and compared to the haunting memory of the 1930s, the economic situation was relatively stable. Instead, the real controversy arose over how to end price and wage controls, causing Truman incredible political trouble. Finding markets for American industries' newfound production capabilities was another priority. Long term plans to promote international free trade, including the Bretton Woods institutions, assuaged these fears.

Like Americans, British citizens were ready to end wartime rations and finally enjoy a peaceful, prosperous lifestyle. Still, the post war reality made that far from possible. Physically, England was in shambles. The blitz had obliterated London, coal was scarce, and the winter of

---

*Report* 32, no. 3 (May/June 2010): 5-8, http://object.cato.org/sites/cato.org/files/serials/files/policy-report/2012/2/cpr32n3-1.pdf.

[32] Gross Domestic Product measures the value of all goods and services produced within a country's borders. The American GDP did not regain 1945 levels until the summer of 1950. David Rosnick, Center for Economic and Policy Research, http://www.cepr.net/index.php/blogs/cepr-blog/clearing-up-some-facts-about-the-depression-of-1946/.

[33] Jack S. Ballard, *The Shock of Peace: Military and Economic Demobilization after World War II* (University Press of America, 1983).

[34] Jason E. Taylor and Richard K. Vedder, "Stimulus by Spending Cuts: Lessons from 1946," *Cato Policy Report* 32, no. 3 (May/June 2010): 5-8, http://object.cato.org/sites/cato.org/files/serials/files/policy-report/2012/2/cpr32n3-1.pdf.

1945-1946 was the coldest anyone could remember. The war's material destruction alone had dramatically altered Britain's landscape, damaging 4,000,000 homes, and rendering over 460,000 of them uninhabitable.[35] Salaries and business profits fell, and food rationing was widespread because the country did not have the purchasing power to finance imports. One British journalist and Labour supporter described the despair in November 1945, writing, "a friend described the middle class last night as 'the suffering classes'."[36] Even citizens who did have the necessary food coupons had to wait in line for hours; "it was queues for everything, you know, even if you didn't know what you were queuing for," one housewife complained.[37] Frustration mounted as British daily life continued to suffer for a war that was supposedly over. Economic reform was of utmost importance in Britain at the end of the war.

Figure 1: Old Bailey Court, 1940

---

[35] G.D.H. Cole, *The Post-war Condition of Britain*, (London: Routledge and Kegan Paul, 1956): 103.
[36] Winston S. Churchill, as quoted in Paul Addison, *Now the War is Over: A Social History of Britain 1945-1951* (London, Jonathan Cape Ltd, 1985), 28.
[37] Mrs. Vera Mather, as quoted by Addison, *Now the War is Over*, 31.

Figure 2: London's Farrington Road, March 8, 1945

This growing sense of financial impotency permeated the English mindset. This impoverishment exacerbated British discontent with their domestic politics. As victors who had sacrificed an uncountable number in the war, British citizens could not understand why austerity measures needed to continue during peacetime. If their enemies were defeated, why did the government need to impose bread rations? Why were many citizens still without employment, homes, or food, despite having sacrificed for their country's victory? Meanwhile, American productivity increased, and British citizens struggled to comprehend how Americans, who had sacrificed fewer men and resources to the war effort, were faring so much better economically. Devastated by the war, British lower classes turned their focus homewards, looking to their government for relief.

Figure 3: Queues of people during the cigarette shortage, 1945

Figure 4: Shoppers lining up for fish, South London, 1945

Thus, popular demand in England for an end to austerity swung political power away

from Churchill and toward Attlee and the Labour party. Churchill the "warmonger" did not have a clear plan for the peacetime Britain, and the lackluster economy mandated government reform. In a populist move, Labour advocated the creation of a welfare state based on the 1942 "Beveridge Report." Although the author, William Beveridge, was a Liberal, Attlee and the Labour party adopted the report's proposals as a concrete prescription for Britain's postwar ills. In fact, Labour politician Ernest Bevin had recommended Beveridge be named chair of the committee, which was in charge of surveying existing social insurance policies, producing the Beveridge Report. Both the Liberal and Labour parties found their power base in the working class, but Liberals had lost all but 12 seats in Parliament by 1945. As a result, the Labour party became the main rival of the Conservative Party and its promotion of laissez-faire economic policies.[38] Labour and its union supporters argued for redistribution of wealth and the "use of the economic assets of the nation for the public good," through welfare policies.[39]

The Beveridge Report outlined a plan to eliminate the five "giant evils" of society: disease, want, ignorance, idleness, and squalor. Beveridge recommended interventionist policies to ensure a certain level of economic equality across Britain. Aneurin Bevan, the future Labour Minister of Health who would create the National Health Service, supported the plan as a "commendable ambition" which could take "the tears…out of capitalism."[40] Bevan explained, "It will still be a battle [against the Conservatives], but we must thank Sir William [Beveridge] for a weapon."[41] The Labour party had found a rallying cry that inspired war weary British voters.

---

[38] "Let U.S. Face the Future," 12.
[39] "Let U.S. Face the Future," 12.
[40] Aneurin Bevan, "Beveridge Manifesto," *Tribune*, December 4, 1942. Bevan would become the Minister of Health under Attlee, serving form 1945-1951.
[41] Bevan, "The Beveridge Manifesto," December 4, 1942.

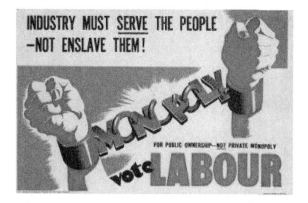

Figure 5: 1945 Labour Campaign poster

During the 1945 election, Labour's socialist platform was based almost entirely on

Beveridge's proposals. In their campaign pamphlet, "Let Us Face the Future," the Labour party

focused on domestic rehabilitation, outlining the need for full employment, the nationalization of

certain industries, protectionist economic policies like price controls, child allowance measures,

and reform of housing, education and health insurance, all policies borrowed from the Beveridge

Report.[42] Politicians recognized the fundamental need for economic vigor to implement such

policies, writing that "there is no good reason why Britain should not afford such programmes,

but she will need full employment and the highest possible industrial efficiency to do so."[43]

American assistance, if continued as expected, could minimize the financial drain of

implementing these policies.

Despite this economic unrest, Labour's win in the 1945 election was not a foregone

conclusion. Churchill was a war hero with international renown, and his defeat was a surprise to

all but the British voters. James Byrnes, the current U.S. Secretary of State, asked Attlee and

Churchill their predictions for the election while the three were at Potsdam, observing that both

---

[42] They advocated nationalizing the fuel, power, iron, steel and inland transport industries, claiming that doing so would lower prices, increase efficiency, and standardize development.

[43] "Let U.S. Face the Future," 10.

candidates "seemed confident that the Conservatives were in by a substantial margin."[44] The

Labour party had only gained national prominence in the 1920s, and Attlee's election marked the

first Labour Parliamentary majority in over a decade. However, voting Labour was a pledge to

fight for economic redistribution, and its promotion of socialism appealed to the needs of its

poorer citizens. As a result, Labour won a huge majority in Parliament, amounting to 393 seats.

Conservatives won 190 seats, and Liberals faded into the background with only 9 seats.

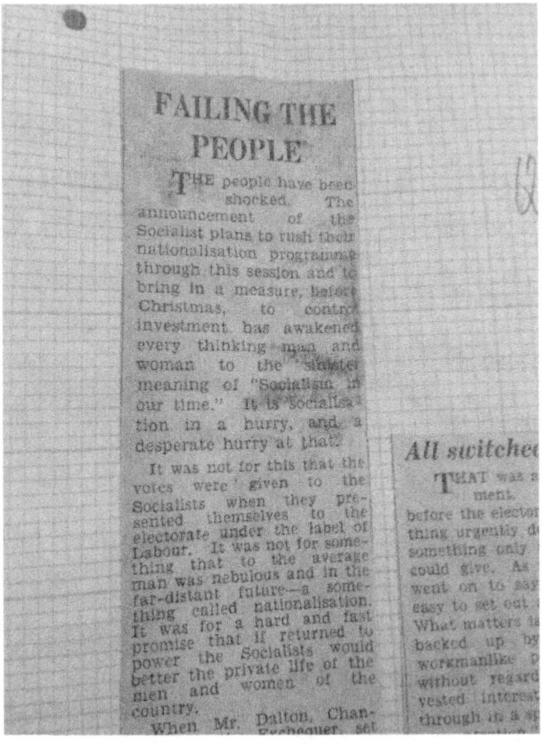

Figure 6: The Labour government's drastic nationalization program provoked substantial
controversy at home and abroad, considered by some British citizens to be "Failing the People,"
"Failing the People," *The Newcastle Journal* (Newcastle upon Tyne), October 9, 1945.
Hugh Dalton Archives, London School of Economics

---

[44] James Byrnes, *All in One Lifetime*, (New York: Harpers & Brothers, 1958), 296.

Attlee's victory publicized Britain's newfound leftist tendencies. In the precarious post-war world, Britain suddenly emerged as the poster child of social welfare and a mixed economy, making the New Deal appear insubstantial in comparison. The Beveridge Report sparked fierce debate in the United States, where an American edition sold over 50,000 copies. Many readers found the principled and egalitarian nature of the Beveridge Report "distinctly American."[45] Attlee's welfare state was even considered "Britain's New Deal."[46] Roosevelt supporters saw "a successful Labour experiment" as an ideal vehicle for an "international extension of the New Deal."[47] However, many Labour members were hostile towards American "Wall Street" culture.[48] Britain's internal debate over welfare policy caused tension between free-enterprise and interventionist American politicians.

Although certain policies, such as the National Health Insurance, had already been introduced before 1945, Britain's embrace of socialism surprised even its own citizens. Sweden and German, her continental neighbors, took on social responsibility much more gradually than Attlee's government did. As Secretary Byrnes had found at Potsdam, British and Americans alike assumed the Conservatives would win. One American journalist even claimed, "the [British] voters not only had short memories; many of them seemed to have political amnesia."[49] The failure of the 1930s Labour government to deal with economic crisis seemed to have been forgotten.[50] More likely, however, English working classes' need for political change reflected economic troubles.

---

[45] Daniel T. Rodgers, *Atlantic Crossings: Social Politics in a Progressive Age* (Cambridge and London: The Belknap Press of Harvard University Press, 1998), 496.

[46] Rodgers, 494.

[47] Theodore Rosenof, "The American Democratic Left looks at the British Labour Government, 1945-1951," (1975), *The Historian* 38, no. 1: 98-100. Fred Block, *The Origins of International Economic Disorder*, 37.

[48] H.C. Allen, *Great Britain and the United States: A History of Anglo-American Relations (1783-1952)*, (New York: St. Martin's Press Inc., 1955), 887-888.

[49] Alan Sked and Chris Cook, *Post-War Britain: A Political History* (New York: Barnes & Noble and Sussex: The Harvester Press, 1979), 18.

[50] Political disputes about whether to increase taxes or cut welfare programs divided the party and

The Labour party had received a mandate to completely rebuild the country, but they found their financial options were limited. Prime Minister Clement Attlee faced a severe crisis in the government's balance of payments immediately upon assuming office. This "melancholy position of Great Britain" stemmed from severe economic disruptions, not just local daily hardships.[51] Britain needed to import goods to end the shortages, but it lacked the adequate dollars or export capabilities to trade with the United States. The short-term focus of wartime economics had justified an immense debt accumulation. Labour campaigners had not considered that Britain could be unable to meet its debt obligations, let alone finance a new welfare program. Politicians had focused on Britain's devastation as a justification for socialism, rather than considering the larger implications of financial turmoil. The Labour campaign pamphlet's declaration, "It is either sound economic controls—or smash," soon proved prophetic.[52]

Prior to the war, Britain had accounted for one fifth of the world's trade, but war reduced its trade by two thirds.[53] Returning to pre-war levels of trade would not be enough to remedy the situation. British "exports would have to be increased to a level 75% above that of 1939" to support its wartime deficit and increased need for imports.[54] In 1946, Britain's national debt stood at a daunting 250% of the country's annual GDP.[55] Despite having defaulted on its commitments to the United States after World War I, Britain had gained a huge new war debt

---

sabotaged its relief efforts. For more information, see: "History of the Labour Party," http://www.labour.org.uk/history_of_the_labour_party.

[51] Peter Clarke, *The Last Thousand Days,* 343.

[52] "Let U.S. Face the Future," 7.

[53] Dean Acheson, U.S. Department of State, "The British Loan—What it Means to Us," (Washington, D.C: Government Printing Office, January 1946): 4. Acheson served under Secretaries of State Edward Stettinius, Jr., James F. Byrnes, and George Marshall, before serving as Secretary of State himself from 1949 to 1953. Regarded by most historians as a fierce Cold Warrior, Acheson was actually criticized by conservative Republicans in 1950 for being "soft" on communism in his support for the Truman Doctrine and Marshall Plan as the primary way to stop the Soviet threat in Europe.

[54] Addison, *Now the War is Over,* 178.

[55] Philip Thornton, "Britain Pays Off Final Installment of U.S. Loan – after 61 Years," *The Independent,* December 29, 2006, http://www.independent.co.uk/news/business/news/britain-pays-off-final-instalment-of-us-loan--after-61-years-430118.html.

under the Lend-Lease act. Its external debts were less than 500 million sterling pounds at the

outbreak of the war, but had increased to 3,355 million pounds in June 1945.[56] England had also

used its empire as a way to secure easy loans, borrowing from India and the former colony of

Egypt to finance the war effort. That alone amounted to 14 billion dollars of debt at the end of

1946.[57] This circular engagement was made possible by Britain's political dominance, the power

of the sterling pound, and advantageous trade regulations. One historian coined this practice as

"hand-to-mouth borrowing," highlighting its inherent conflict with free trade.[58] For example,

Britain established a Sterling Area dollar pool in 1939, where countries that used pound sterling

or currencies pegged to it (basically Britain and its dependencies) combined their dollar deposits

in London and could draw on it to meet deficit obligations to countries that used dollar-based

currencies.[59] Member countries benefited from being able to trade amongst themselves without

exchange controls and from London's financial backing. After the war, it was more difficult for a

weakened Britain to extract wealth from its increasingly restive and independence-minded

colonies, but the Sterling Area remained a way to protect the international value its currency.

---

[56] Cole, 102.
[57] Fred Vinson, U.S. Department of State, "The British Loan—What it Means to Us," (Washington, D.C: Government Printing Office, January 1946): 4.
[58] Peter Clarke, *The Last Thousand Days,* 375.
[59] In 1939, the Sterling Area included all of the British colonies and dependencies except Canada, Newfoundland, and Hong Kong. Kenneth M. Wright, "Dollar Pooling in the Sterling Area, 1939-1952" *The American Economic Review* 44, no. 4 (September 1954): 559-576, http://www.jstor.org/stable/1814109.

Figure 7: "Britain and refugees"
French President Charles de Gaulle and U.S. President Harry Truman hand off the colonies to Britannia after the war.
Leslie Gilbert Illingworth, *The Daily Mail* (London), October 3, 1945.[60]
The National Library of Wales.

Soon, England's debt had grown to such an extent that famous economist Lord John Maynard Keynes warned of an impending "financial Dunkirk," comparing the crisis to the June 1940 battle when the British army was barely evacuated from what Churchill called "a colossal military disaster."[61] In August 1945, Keynes argued before Parliament that if these economic issues went unaddressed, "there would have to be an indefinite postponement of the realization of the best hopes of the new [Labour] Government."[62] Before Prime Minister Clement Attlee

---

[60] Leslie Gilbert Illingworth was a cartoonist for *Punch* Magazine and *The Daily Mail*. For more information, see: "Leslie Gilbert Illingworth," British Cartoon Archive Biographies, http://www.cartoons.ac.uk/artists/leslie-gilbertillingworth/biography,
[61] Winston Churchill, "We Shall Fight in the Beaches," (Speech, London, The House of Commons, June 4, 1940), http://www.churchill-society-london.org.uk/Dunkirk.html.

could implement his new policies, he needed to cure the country's debilitating economic situation. Not only did he plan to finance his ambitious domestic social agenda, but he also had to reestablish Britain's international economic prowess from before the war to maintain its status as a world power. According to Keynes, Britain's only options were continued austerity measures, escalated borrowing from the colonies, or a renewed loan from the United States. Keynes's speech forced the Attlee government to come to terms with the dire nature of their situation. It was obvious that the country was financially incapacitated, but Keynes drove the message home and convinced Parliamentarians that the United States' prosperity was its last source of hope. Six days later, Foreign Secretary Ernest Bevin claimed, "Never was there a time when economic reconstruction was so vital to foreign policy and international co-operation as now."[63] The first test of the new Labour government would be one of fiscal survival.

[62] Lord Keynes, "Our Overseas Financial Prospects," (Speech, London, The House of Commons, August 14, 1945), King's College Cambridge, J.M.K. Papers.
[63] Ernest Bevin, (Speech, London, The House of Commons, August 20, 1945), King's College Cambridge, J.M.K. Papers

Figure 8: John Maynard Keynes

Political controversy within the United States itself contributed to confusion over how to interpret Britain's political and economic situation. Americans had just lost Franklin Delano Roosevelt, who led the New Deal coalition from 1933 until his death in April 1945. Just as Churchill had recently dominated British politics, Roosevelt had been many Americans' inspiration during the tumultuous years of the Great Depression and World War II. Suddenly Harry Truman, relatively unknown to the public and surprisingly unaware of many current issues, became President. The day after Roosevelt's death, Truman voiced his trepidation to reporters, "Boys, if you ever pray, pray for me now. I don't know if you fellas ever had a load of hay fall on you, but when they told me what happened yesterday, I felt like the moon, the stars, and all the planets had fallen on me."[64] For example, Truman did not know about the Manhattan Project, which had begun in 1939 and was well underway by the time he took office. Truman's brief 82-day stint as Vice President offered less than adequate preparation for the duties of a post-war President.

As a result, Truman had trouble navigating the American transition to peace. After the war, popular discontent with the Truman administration caused his approval rating to plummet. In June 1946, 48% of Americans said they would not vote for him as a candidate in 1948, and 46% of Americans disapproved of the way his administration was handling foreign affairs.[65] Roosevelt and Truman had not discussed post-war plans, and Truman's policies faced a constant comparison against those of the late President.[66] Truman's loss of support came in large part

---

[64] Harry S. Truman, as quoted in "Harry S. Truman: His Life and Times" (Harry S. Truman Library and Museum), http://www.trumanlibrary.org/lifetimes/whouse.htm.

[65] Gallup Poll (AIPO), June 1-6, 1946, Roper Center Public Opinion Archives.

[66] William E. Leuchtenburg, "New Faces of 1946," *Smithsonian Magazine* (November 2006), http://www.smithsonianmag.com/history/new-faces-of-1946-135190660/?no-ist.

from his inability to keep prices down when consumer demand largely outweighed consumer goods.[67] As the labor supply outpaced the growing economy, wages fell and led to the 1946 labor union strikes, the largest in the United States to date. 116 million man-labor days were lost, more than three times any previous record.[68] The New Deal Coalition began to weaken after Roosevelt's death, and Truman struggled to lead the nation, both economically and politically. It was in this contentious environment that the economic disaster in England had to be considered, explaining why many American politicians were unenthusiastic about making financial commitments to Britain. The domestic economy was Truman's main priority.

As a result, with the support of Congress, Truman abruptly ended Lend-Lease aid to Britain after V-J day in August 1945. This move shocked many British politicians who assumed that aid would continue at least until the end of the year. Attlee articulated the situation in his diary, writing, "We weren't in a position to bargain…when the end of the war brought the end of Lend Lease it was made as black as it could possibly be. We'd used up all our resources. We'd allowed the Americans to have all kinds of export trades that we used to have. We'd emptied the till of our foreign investments…we had to get our exports going. When they cut off Lend Lease we were given a body blow."[69] Americans considered the alliance unnecessary with the end of the war, while the British regarded the partnership more relevant than ever. The sudden termination of Lend-Lease made clear the extent of British dependence on American economic support and the shift in economic power across the Atlantic. The Anglo-American alliance was more internationally recognized than ever, yet each country's efforts at dominance after the war deeply threatened its existence. Britain sought to maintain its empire and to promote the status of

---

[67] Leuchtenburg, "New Faces of 1946."

[68] Leuchtenburg, "New Faces of 1946."

[69] Clement Attlee, recorded by Francis Williams, *Twilight of Empire*, (New York: A.S. Barnes & Co., 1962), 134. Quoted by Gardner, *Architects*, 123.

sterling at all costs, and the United States wanted political and economic influence by encouraging capitalism and free trade around the world. Still, neither country could abandon the other without ending an alliance that had defined international politics since World War I and creating a dangerous political vacuum in the post-war world.

World War II had offered an opportunity for renegotiating the world order. The growing disconnect between American and British perspectives, as exemplified in British assumptions of continued aid and American efforts at economic demobilization, was most apparent in regard to international economics. Trade policies enacted by Britain in response to the Great Depression and World War II had given it substantial control of trade within both its colonial empire and with other countries whose currencies were pegged to the sterling pound, such as Egypt and Sweden.[70] In 1932, partly in response to the American Smoot-Hawley Act, the British formalized its Imperial Preference system for the Sterling-area countries.[71] Under this system, Britain enacted high tariffs to discourage trading outside the Sterling Area. To conserve dollars for the purchase of munitions, Britain also created the Sterling Area dollar pool. These arrangements gave Britain considerable control over the dollar trade of the Sterling Area, an advantage which it was reluctant to give up after the war ended its primary justification. Britain also made sterling assets non-convertible into other currencies, forcing countries with large sterling reserves to trade mainly with sterling-based economies.[72]

---

[70] The importance of British control of the Sterling Area is demonstrated by the fact that sterling was used for 36 percent of all world trade in 1950. See: Curt Cardwell, *NSC 68 and the Political Economy of the Early Cold War* (Cambridge University Press, 2011): 131; Edward H. Collins, "Economics and Finance: 'The Dollar Gap' – Gone or Just Obscured?" *The New York Times,* November 27, 1950, 45.

[71] *The Sterling Area* (British Information Services, 1945), 5. The Smoot-Hawley Act of June 1930 raised tariffs on over 200,000 goods to historic levels.

[72] Curt Cardwell, *NSC 68 and the Political Economy of the Early Cold War* (Cambridge University Press, 2011): 131-132.

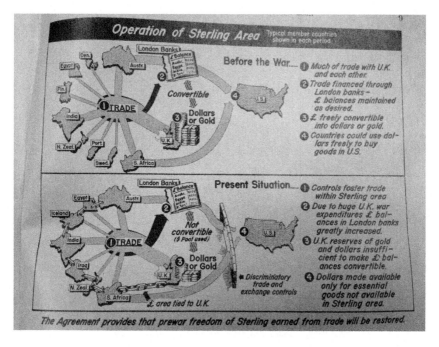

Figure 9: "Operation of the Sterling Area."
U.S. State Department Pamphlet on the loan explains the British Sterling Area.
"International Trade and the British Loan," Washington, D.C., U.S. Department of State, 1946

Prior to World War II, a triangular international trade arrangement existed: The United

States imported raw materials from Asian markets and sold goods to Europe, who would in turn

transfer much of its goods and non-tangible services (such as foreign investments, shipping

services, tourism) to Asia.[73] The war disrupted this system, as the U.S. began to import from

Latin America rather than Europe, and Europe no longer had any export surpluses to finance its

deficit with the U.S.[74] This shift, combined with increased agitation in India and Burma, made

the British fearful about how to export enough goods to finance its economy. In the view of

---

[73] Fred Block, *The Origins of International Economic Disorder: A Study of United States International Monetary Policy from World War II to the Present* (Berkeley, Los Angeles, and London: University of California Press, 1977), 79.
[74] Block, 79.

many British politicians, maintaining preferential trading within the Sterling Area gave Britain protection from the harsh realities of free trade.

Inflationary pressures in the United Kingdom also raised fears of open trade, for, as economist Fred Block explains, "if trade were to proceed on an open basis, with any kind of reasonable exchange rates, all of the high-inflation countries would be deluged by goods from the low-inflation countries, and the high-inflation countries would be in serious balance of payments trouble."[75] In other words, Britain would import more goods than it could afford, since its exports would be too expensive for other countries to purchase. These concerns caused a reactionary dedication to what one American *Foreign Affairs* journalist termed "ultra-protectionism."[76] Britain enjoyed status and economic clout as a result of this protectionist system, which it wanted to preserve, despite its extreme burden of war debt. The policies supported the political strength of the empire and shielded it from competition with American exports.

American economists and businessmen found the imperial preference system and Sterling Area dollar pool insulting to their own economic worldview. Commercially, they also wanted access to British imperial materials and markets, which would be key customers for American industries. During the war, the Americans had developed a specific vision for a post-war international system. Representatives from the Allied nations gathered at a resort in Bretton Woods, New Hampshire, in July 1944. They sought to avoid repeating the economic disruptions

---

[75] Block, 78.

[76] Herbert Feis, "The Future of British Imperial Preferences," *Foreign Affairs Quarterly* 24 (July 1946), http://www.foreignaffairs.com/articles/70525/herbert-feis/the-future-of-british-imperial-preferences. Feis previously worked in the State Department as an economic advisor and criticized his superiors for not alternatives to "rigid formulas" in its protesting Russian trade agreements with satellite countries. See also: Feis, "The Conflict over Trade Ideologies," *Foreign Affairs Quarterly* 25 (January 1947): 217-228 http://www.foreignaffairs.com/articles/70559/herbert-feis/the-conflict-over-trade-ideologies and Feis, "Keynes in Retrospect," *Foreign Affairs Quarterly* 29 (July 1951): 564-577, http://www.foreignaffairs.com/articles/70903/herbert-feis/keynes-in-retrospect.

that followed the First World War. Their discussions created a monetary system in which most currencies would be pegged to the dollar, with the dollar nominally backed by gold.[77] In addition, the agreements created the International Monetary Fund, which oversees its member nations' currencies and exchange rates and lends to countries with balance-of-payments problems. The agreements also founded the International Bank for Reconstruction and Development (later called the World Bank), which would provide loans for infrastructure in developing countries to promote economic development. These Bretton Woods agreements would open world markets to the American industrial export powerhouse. The easy convertibility of currencies would dramatically simplify international trade, while establishing the dollar as the world's primary reserve currency.

At the time Britain asked the United States for a loan, she had not yet ratified Bretton Woods. The United Kingdom was unwilling to abandon its advantageous system of Imperial Preferences and limited convertibility of the pound outside the Sterling Area. American capitalists saw this loan as a chance to compel Britain into the Bretton Woods agreement. Britain considered this loan as their last chance to get funding from the United States on favorable terms not subject to the requirements of the Bretton Woods institutions. It was in this context that British diplomats arrived in Washington to request American economic assistance.

---

[77] In 1933, the U.S. Government outlawed private gold ownership, consolidating it all in the U.S. Treasury. This was an effective abandonment of the gold standard. However, the government also committed to converting dollars into gold at $35 per ounce for foreign governments and central banks, which supported the dollar as a reliable reserve currency.

Figure 10: Lord Halifax

In September 1945, Attlee dispatched economist John Maynard Keynes and Edward Wood, the Lord of Halifax and ambassador to the United States, to negotiate a grant to rescue and stabilize the British economy.[78] The loan that resulted would an assessment of America's willingness to resist isolationism and embrace large and expensive overseas commitments. It was the key point in determining how the United States would manage its newfound economic and political power. In one 1946 *New York Times* article entitled "Loan to Britain Tests Our New World Role," the author claimed "Americans cannot see beyond their own noses."[79] The question remained whether the United States would accept (and potentially abuse) its new international responsibility and whether Britain could cope with its dissipating power. The

---

[78] Halifax was Neville Chamberlain's Foreign Secretary, Viceroy of India from 1926-1931 and was famously passed over in favor of Churchill as Prime Minister in 1940.
[79] John H. Crider, "Loan to Britain Tests Our New World Role," *The New York Times,* April 27, 1946, http://query.nytimes.com/mem/archive/pdf?res=F10710FD3C5B127A93CAAB178FD85F428485F9.

Anglo-American relationship had been challenged, and the uncertainty of the postwar world

presented an opportunity to reevaluate its balance of power.

## Chapter Two: The Negotiations

In Washington Lord Halifax
Once whispered to Lord Keynes:
"It's true *they* have the money bags
But *we* have all the brains."[80]

This political joke between the British Ambassador to the United States and his leading

economist during post war negotiations reveals how Keynes and Halifax underestimated the

difficulty of their mission. The Keynes-Halifax financial appeal of September 1945 advertised to

the Americans the dire economic circumstances of Britain. By this time, Britain's financial

situation had become untenable. Options for financing the economy, let alone the Attlee

government's ambitious social welfare agenda, were dwindling. John Maynard Keynes's

argument for U.S. assistance had gained substantial traction among Labour politicians.

Increasing British exports was not feasible considering the country's incapacitated industries,

and the United Kingdom was already substantially indebted to South America, Egypt, and India,

which had provided Britain with easy loans during the war. Only the Anglo-American alliance

offered a (seemingly) friendly face in the hostile realm of post-war international relations. A few

weeks after Keynes's convincing speech to Parliament on August 14, 1945, he and Halifax left

for the United States, and the negotiations that ensued would result in the Anglo-American Loan

of 1946.

Keynes was confident that he would be able to secure a large credit to tide the country

over until levels of production reached prewar standards. In fact, he so convinced Parliament of

his ability to procure assistance that Foreign Secretary Bevin said: "When I listen to Lord

Keynes talking…I seem to hear those coins jingling in my pocket; but I am not so sure that they

---

[80] Anonymous, as quoted in Gardner, *Sterling-Dollar Diplomacy*, xxiii. According to Gardner, the verse was found on "a yellowing piece of paper salvaged from the first Anglo-American discussions during World War II about postwar economic arrangements."

are really there."[81] Bevin's premonition that the United States may not want to give Britain as much aid as Keynes expected was perceptive. However, Keynes did not approach the negotiations without hesitation. Although outwardly confident, Keynes wrote to Halifax that this trip would "prove, I think, the toughest negotiation of all."[82] Keynes knew that broaching a potential loan would inherently entail discussions of Bretton Woods, ending Lend-Lease, and overarching commercial policies.[83] This Pandora's Box would "doubtless" be "the price of their [American] assistance," Keynes wrote.[84] As one scholar explained, "London had to ensure that it did not just become Washington's appendage."[85] Economic partnership would always come with certain concessions, but the question remained whether the wartime alliance would make the Americans more generous.

Figure 11: Henry Morgenthau, US Secretary of Treasury, and John Maynard Keynes
Bretton Woods Conference, July 1944

Keynes and his colleagues assumed that because of Britain's substantial losses in the war and its pivotal role in the Allied victory, the United States would have no choice but to honor its ally in her time of need. Britain had sacrificed three times as many people in the war as the

[81] Harrod, *Life of John Maynard Keynes,* 596.
[82] John Maynard Keynes, Letter to Halifax from Keynes, August 17, 1945, King's College Cambridge, J.M.K. Papers.
[83] Keynes, Letter to Halifax from Keynes, August 17, 1945, King's College Cambridge, J.M.K. Papers.
[84] Keynes, Letter to Halifax from Keynes, August 17, 1945, King's College Cambridge, J.M.K. Papers.
[85] Ovendale, 19.

United States, losses that amounted to almost 1% of its entire 1939 population.[86] The martyrdom of Britain would obligate the Americans to support her, or so many Parliamentarians thought. Keynes was so convinced that a grant would feasible that he argued he "should not be authorized to agree to anything except an out-and-out grant. Help on any less favourable terms should not be accepted."[87] There was no discussion of what would happen if the Americans refused.

As the main proponent of American aid and an established royal economist, John Maynard Keynes was a natural choice to lead the negotiations with the United States. Keynes even requested the discussions be held in Washington rather than London because he could best negotiate a deal away from the meddlesome members of Parliament, whose diverse opinions and political alliances could jeopardize his bargaining power.[88] To accompany him, Attlee sent Lord Halifax, a Conservative politician who had previously served as Viceroy of India and Foreign Secretary before becoming the American Ambassador in 1941. Halifax had plenty of experience negotiating between foreign governments. By 1942, however, Halifax requested an early retirement following his son's premature death. In addition, Halifax did not have a good relationship with Roosevelt and maintained a relatively low profile in the United States. The loan negotiations marked the end of his political career; he would retire in 1946. As a result, from their arrival on September 11, 1945, Keynes ran the show.

Despite his qualifications, Keynes's assumptions regarding American sentiments were far from the truth. Most Americans did not support giving Britain a loan as a sign of appreciation,

---

[86] Britain had sacrificed .94% of its 1939 population; The United States had sacrificed .32% of its 1939 population.

[87] *The Collected Writings of John Maynard Keynes XXIV: Activities 1944-1946: The Transition to Peace*, (Cambridge, U.K.: Cambridge University Press, 1979, 2003), 421.

[88] During the Great Depression, Labour Prime Minister Ramsay MacDonald supported classical economics policies, which advocated a free market with little regulation. Because of his administration's limited economic knowledge, they were blamed in large part for Britain's troubles. This trend continued into Attlee's administration, which was only the third Labour government in power – still unproven even to its own citizens. Keynes was a revered economist and a member of the struggling Liberal Party. His policies filled a void in Labour foreign economic policy.

much less free money in the form of a grant. The Great Depression was a far from distant memory, and the uncertainty of the post-war economy made American public opinion vehemently opposed to lending foreign powers money, even to its closest ally. Precisely at the time of the Keynes-Halifax mission, 60% of Americans ardently disapproved of a loan of three to five billion dollars to help England get back to its feet.[89] Clearly, Keynes and the British government did not have an accurate perspective of how their ambitious proposal would be received.

By sending Keynes and Halifax to consult with the United States less than a month after the end of Lend-Lease, Britain allowed the Americans to turn the situation to their advantage. Lend-Lease had set a precedent of American support for the British economy, and an extension of that aid seemed sensible, especially in light of Britain's extenuating circumstances. Lend-Lease's extremely easy terms had muddled British expectations. When discussing the loan with American negotiators, Keynes asked, "Can't you have another brain-wave like Lend-Lease to get us out of our difficulties?" The American response was a blunt "No. Sir, we're not having any more brain-waves."[90] British politicians soon realized that this new loan would not come easily. Political alliance was no longer enough to validate substantial American aid.

---

[89] Gallup Poll (AIPO), September 8-13, 1945, Roper Center Public Opinion Archives.
[90] Keynes and American negotiators as quoted in "Sterling-Dollar Diplomacy," *The Economic Weekly*, August 4, 1956.

<u>Figure 12</u>: William Clayton

The American negotiators were Will Clayton, a cotton trader and Assistant Secretary of State for economic affairs, and Fred Vinson, a Kentucky Democrat serving as Secretary of the Treasury. They were advised by Winthrop Aldrich, president of Chase Bank and Ambassador to the United Kingdom, who emphasized the need to demolish the Sterling Area, imperial preferences, and exchange controls to support the growth of American businesses. The choice of these men as negotiators reveals the power of U.S. business interests in dictating economic policy, another fact that British politicians had not anticipated.

Will Clayton was a cotton king, Southerner, and free trade enthusiast. He had a "natural charm," *Time Magazine* reported, despite many Americans' resentment of his success in the cotton industry.[91] In fact, his founding of the Anderson, Clayton, and Company made him the

"the biggest cotton merchant in the world" prior to the war.[92] Politically, Clayton had been a

Liberty Leaguer, opposing Roosevelt's New Deal because of the Agricultural Adjustment Act's

support of the agricultural market.[93] In August 1936, Clayton, who would become Truman's

Undersecretary of State, told *Time* magazine that while he was a Democrat he was adamantly not

a "New Deal Democrat."[94] However, he left the Liberty League after only one year of

membership and came to support Roosevelt once the Administration began to advocate a

multilateral, free trade policy under Secretary of State Cordell Hull's leadership.[95] Above all,

Clayton was "by training, tradition, and conviction...a free trader. Any meddling with the

economic machine is, to him, the supreme sin."[96] He soon owned the largest cotton-trading

enterprise, after expanding to Latin America and Egypt.[97] Clayton's interest in international

economics persisted, and in 1944, Clayton became Assistant Secretary for Economic Affairs.

---

[91] "Business: Cotton is King," *Time Magazine*, August 17, 1936,
http://content.time.com/time/subscriber/article/0,33009,756494-2,00.html.
[92] "Business: Cotton is King."
[93] Texas State Historical Association, http://www.tshaonline.org/handbook/online/articles/fcl23.
[94] "Business: Cotton is King," *Time Magazine*, August 17, 1936,
http://content.time.com/time/subscriber/article/0,33009,756494-2,00.html.
[95] He joined the Liberty League in 1934 but left in 1935 "when it failed to accept his recommendations for public relations in Texas." For more information, see: Texas State Historical Association,
http://www.tshaonline.org/handbook/online/articles/fcl23.
[96] "Business: Cotton is King."
[97] He built fourteen cotton oil mills and seventy-five cotton gins in Brazil, Mexico, Argentina, Peru, Paraguay and Egypt. See: Gardner, *Architects,* 116.

Figure 13: Fred Vinson

Like Clayton, co-negotiator Fred Vinson was a Southerner with strong business priorities. A Kentucky Democrat, he strongly supported the priorities of the Truman administration. Despite his economic role in the Treasury, Vinson was a lawyer by training and would be appointed to Chief Justice of the U.S. Supreme Court in June 1946 after a yearlong stint in Treasury. Keynes commented on the prevalence of American lawyers during the negotiations, in contrast with his own mission's lack thereof. The American team was not risking its judgment with illusions of partnership, while the British had arrived empty-handed, desperate, and trusting. This combination of legal and business interests (like Vinson and Clayton) manifested itself throughout the entire negotiations.

As one scholar explained, "If Clayton played ball, it would be because the British delivered on his multilateral trade agenda, despite the Empire; and if Vinson played ball, it would be because he was sure that it was the kind of package that he could sell to Congress."[98] Clayton considered the loan an opportunity to push own interests, as a cotton exporter who supported eliminating trade barriers that would keep other countries from importing his cotton. Meanwhile, Vinson approached the negotiations as "a straight business deal, [considering] it…his duty not to permit the brilliant, fast-talking economist with the careless airs of a Cambridge don to put anything over on the American squares."[99] Vinson and Keynes did not get along and even made fun of each other during the meetings.[100] The negotiations became a much more spirited and contentious debate than the British had previously expected.

The negotiations opened with presentations from the British envoys in Washington. For three days, Keynes and Halifax testified to the Federal Reserve, explaining the extent of Britain's economic crisis, hoping to garner American sympathy for their plight. Subsequent rounds took the shape of a back and forth between different potential proposals. On October 18, 1945, Clayton offered a $5 billion loan at 2% interest over fifty years, and Parliament turned it down flat, since British politicians still held hope for an interest-free grant.[101] Later, on November 5, 1945, Chancellor of the Exchequer Hugh Dalton introduced his own proposals to the Americans, offering many of the concessions that would constitute the final agreement reached in December.[102]

These rounds were tough, and each side belittled the other. Keynes and Halifax sent telegrams code-named NABOBS back to a team of British officials in Parliament (including

---

[98] Peter Clarke, *The Last Thousand Days,* 393.

[99] Bert Cochran, *Harry Truman and the Crisis Presidency* (New York: Funk & Wagnalls, 1973), 191-2.

[100] Edmonds, 100. See also: Harrod, *Keynes,* 597, 604, 612, and 627; Gardner, *Sterling-Dollar Diplomacy,* 201.

[101]Peter Clarke, *The Last Thousand Days,* 394.

[102] Hugh Dalton, "Washington Financial Talks," The National Archives CAB 129/5/12, November 28, 1945, 2.

Dalton, Foreign Secretary Ernest Bevin, and President of the Board of Trade Stafford Cripps) during their Washington meetings, only to receive replies that were humorously referred to as BABOONS.[103] This wisecrack highlights British disrespect for the Americans who were negotiating the loan. The Americans were similarly contemptuous. After the negotiations Will Clayton boasted to financier Bernard Baruch that "We loaded the British loan negotiations with all the conditions the traffic would bear."[104] Mutual respect had taken a backseat to personal interest.

The American team was almost entirely preoccupied by the stipulations that could be tied to the loan, rather than the loan itself. Even before Britain introduced its proposal, Clayton had considered proposing an extension of lend-lease if Britain "signed up to the multilateral agenda – coupled with the warning that there were bound to be strings."[105] Lending money was not the issue, but rather what particular American constituencies (such as businessmen like Clayton) could stand to gain. Clayton had no qualms revealing this agenda to the British, saying, "…if you succeed in doing away with the Empire preference and opening up the Empire to U.S. Commerce, it may well be that we can afford to pay a couple of billion dollars for the privilege."[106] For Clayton and Vinson, the goal of the loan was not to help the British, but to promote American trade. This would serve the interests of American capitalists, and it would also solve the problem of finding customers to meet American industries' wartime production capabilities.

It was for this reason that Keynes and Halifax's primary strategy of emotional appeal to Americans failed. Only three percent of Americans found the recent military alliance a convincing argument for granting Britain a loan.[107] Anglophobia was prevalent. Non-

---

[103]Peter Clarke, *The Last Thousand Days,* 380.
[104] Cochran, 192.
[105]Peter Clarke, *The Last Thousand Days,* 372.
[106] Clayton as quoted in "Sterling-Dollar Diplomacy," *The Economic Weekly*, August 4, 1956.
[107] Gallup Poll (AIPO), March 29-April 3, 1946, Roper Center Public Opinion Archives.

interventionists resented Churchill for his strategic appeals to the U.S. at the outset of the war, blaming him for their country's involvement in foreign wars. An anonymous woman even sent Churchill a letter during one of his repeated trips to the United States in 1942, saying, "Every time you appear on our shores, it means something very terrible for us. Why do you not stay at home and fight your own battles instead of always pulling us into them to save your rotten neck? You are taking foul advantage of our blithering idiot of a president."[108] Many Americans were exasperated with Britain and its never-ending appeals for assistance. Europe seemed like a distant place that continued to entangle the U.S. in its messy affairs.

This mistrust of the United Kingdom was widespread across both political parties. In particular, the Labour Party's election in July 1945 struck fear in conservative Americans. The defeated British Conservatives, despite their acceptance of the Beveridge Plan's fundamentals, blasted the Labour agenda and "lumped these policies all together as the 'road to serfdom'...[claiming that] England had gone 'red' and 'radical'."[109] The American public began to compare British Labour policies with the Soviet Union, a dangerous association at the outset of the Cold War. The more serious implications of the comparison failed to materialize, for socialist hopes "that left would be more easily able to speak with left in other countries...faded rapidly" as British negotiations with Russia soon became frigid.[110] However, the threat of socialism to traditional American individualism weakened American support for the Labour government in Britain.

Lending the British money would be an implicit approval of Attlee's socialist agenda, since London could use the assistance to support its socialist policies.[111] Conservative Americans

---

[108] Letter to Churchill intercepted by the FBI, June 19, 1942. "Churchill and U.S. Entry into World War II," http://www.ihr.org/jhr/v09/v09p261_Irving.html
[109] Rodgers, 493.
[110] Ovendale, 17.
[111] Ovendale, 20.

criticized Clement Attlee's appeal for a socialist welfare state as an encroachment on free enterprise, disregarding how desperate British citizens were for necessities like basic shelter, healthcare, and even food. For many Labour supporters (who often compromised of poorer union workers), Attlee's election was not a matter of idealism but rather the result of a frantic search for stability and peace. Attlee offered a safety net for his struggling constituents by implementing unemployment benefits, creating a national health insurance, and nationalizing industries. Still, in the United States, Labour's sweeping reforms raised fears of socialism, forcing Americans to consider how much their own government's role had evolved during the recent New Deal.

In 1945, Democrats controlled the presidency and both houses. Republicans had not been in power since losing over 100 seats in the House, 12 seats in the Senate, and the Presidency in 1932. Despite their longstanding electoral success, the Democrats were internally divided between Southern rural conservatives and the Northern industrial liberals. Roosevelt had managed to keep both wings in the Democratic coalition, but Truman struggled to keep both liberal and conservative Democrats together. One contention included Roosevelt New Dealers who were similar to British Labour supporters in their economic views. Secretary of Commerce Henry Wallace, Roosevelt's former Vice President, an extreme liberal who proposed his own global New Deal Plans, was one such supporter of Attlee's victory. Other Democrats, like Clayton, were economically conservative free traders. He advocated support for Britain only on specific free trade terms. While both Wallace and Clayton recommended a loan for the Labour government, they did so for very different reasons.

Truman and the negotiators needed to address this public resentment of continued assistance for Britain. In order to pass a loan through Congress, the deal had to seem particularly advantageous for the United States economy. Clayton realized that the loan and Britain's participation in free trade policies were interdependent and considered this his chance to push his economic agenda. Since Britain had considerable control over the trade of its colonies and other Sterling-based economies, a change in its economic policies could open their markets to the United States. Ever the businessman, Clayton "had learned that he had to resuscitate the customer before he could hope to do business with him."[112] Only when Britain was stable financially could it do away with its protectionist measures; and only when it did away with those measures would American trade benefit.

Clayton's concerns for multilateralism were warranted. The United States worried over how to maintain its economic growth after the war. The United States had dramatically increased its exports from four billion dollars before the war to fifteen billion dollars, according to the *President's Economic Report for 1946.* Clark Clifford, later Secretary of Defense during the Vietnam War, argued that "intense demand of foreign countries for goods available only, or chiefly, in the United States has become one of the factors sustaining a high level of employment, production and purchasing power in the U.S. as government expenditures declined."[113] The country needed substantial markets to sustain this level of exports. If Britain could not afford to import, the United States would be losing a huge customer.

These trade concerns led Clayton and Vinson to suggest much of the "fine print" of the loan's provisions. In return for assistance, Britain agreed to dramatically reduce its system of imperial preference, end currency exchange controls to make the pound sterling convertible, and to pass the Bretton Woods proposal. All of these policies promoted Clayton's goals of international collaboration and free trade, but also opened the vast British Empire to American goods. The British were forced to reduce the Sterling Area trade preferences, which the U.S.

---

[112] Cochran, 192.
[113] *President's Economic Report for 1946,* mimeographed copy in Harry S. Truman Papers, Files of Clark M. Clifford, Box 4, dated January 8, 1947, 50.

considered an impediment to free trade. However, that also meant giving up the commerce that gave cohesion to its empire and strength to the sterling. The loan had become an impetus for talks on the entire international trade system.

The requirement for Britain to end the currency exchange controls meant the reinstatement of sterling convertibility.[114] Immediately upon Congress's passage of the loan, Britain would be required to implement convertibility into dollars on "day-to-day business transactions with Americans."[115] Undersecretary of State Dean Acheson explained that this pegging to the dollar "meant that an American manufacturer who has sold his goods to Great Britain will be able to collect his proceeds in dollars."[116] This would be an immediate benefit for men like cotton trader Will Clayton. The loan also required that Britain implement international convertibility by one year from the loan's passage. Acheson used this requirement to fight accusations that the multilateral goals were self-serving, saying, "I should add that under the terms of the agreement, at the end of the year no restrictions will be imposed by the British on day-to-day transactions in *any* part of the world."[117] Sterling would be convertible to any currency for any merchant, facilitating trade around the globe. This ended the sterling-area dollar pool and allowed many of Britain's creditors (such as India) to draw on their reserves in dollars rather than in pound sterling.

---

[114] Prior to World War I, Britain and the United States had both used the gold standard, which effectively resulted in a fixed exchange rate between the two currencies. Both countries abandoned the standard to finance WWI. In Britain, despite a brief reinstatement from 1925-1931, it was rendered moot by the Great Depression. Likewise, President Roosevelt weakened the standard in 1933 by ending gold-payment contracts and nationalized private citizens' gold. The U.S. dollar was no longer convertible into gold beginning in 1971 under President Richard Nixon.

[115] Acheson, 6.

[116] Acheson, 6.

[117] Acheson, 6-7.

Figure 14: "The Babes in Bretton Wood"
Keynes and Halifax encounter frightening figures representing Wall Street and Congress. Bretton Wood refers to the inclusion of many Bretton Woods stipulations in the loan requirements. David Low, *The Evening Standard* (London), November 27, 1945.

In order to receive the loan proceeds, Britain also needed to join the International Monetary Fund and World Bank, which were created by the Bretton Woods International Agreement of 1944. Until the loan, Britain had resisted signing this agreement because it created an international economic system with the U.S. at the center and required dismantling most of the Sterling Area trade preferences. In fact, many of the previously mentioned 1946 loan obligations were also prerequisites for membership in the Bretton Woods institutions. For example, when the 1946 loan's requirement for free trade practices expired in December 1951, Britain would still be unable to impose restrictions on payments or transfers under the International Monetary Fund agreement. The loan agreement also imposed a harsher one-year transition period for sterling-dollar convertibility than the IMF agreement, which gave other Fund signatories the luxury of five years to pin their currencies to a floating exchange rate. In this way, the loan was an expedited version of many of the Bretton Woods requirements.

The Americans also insisted that the loan have interest payments, which would make it easier for Congress to approve. A loan was a much easier sell to the American public than a grant. However, this was also the most contentious issue for the British. Politicians had expected an interest-free grant and were extremely insulted when this was not offered. For this reason, Keynes and Halifax had been most assertive during the discussions of the loan's payment terms. A compromise was reached, and the loan would be interest free for 6 years, with a comparatively low 2% interest rate that would be paid over a fifty-year term. The agreement also included a stipulation that under certain circumstances, Britain would be able to waive her interest payments. This generous allowance noted that the waived payments would not be postponed, but rather wiped from the books. Still, these certain circumstances were defined by "automatic criterion," not a case-by-case basis, limiting the autonomy of the British government in determining when a waiver would be necessary.[118] These automatic criterion were actually proposed by Chancellor of the Exchequer Hugh Dalton in a telegram on November 6, 1945, and consisted "in the event of…a breakdown of multilateral clearing, an international depression of trade, or a scarcity of dollars" and "in the event of United Kingdom exports failing in any year to reach an agreed

---

[118] The British government waived its interest payments on the loan six times "on the grounds that the international exchange rate conditions and the United Kingdom's foreign currency reserves made payment impractical" according to the *Independent* article "Britain Pays Off Final Installment of U.S. Loan after 61 years." The deferment years were 1956, 1957, 1964, 1965, 1968, and 1976.

[118] Acheson, 9.

target."[119] However, it is unlikely Dalton expected the United States (rather than Britain) would have the power to monitor these events. Both Labour and Conservative politicians worried about the paradox of taking on more debt to finance their pre-existing indebted decision, but these relatively easy repayment terms helped ease their fears.

Clayton and Vinson were also concerned about Britain's immense foreign debt, but for different reasons. They wanted assurance that the service of this loan would have priority over other obligations. As a result, the United Kingdom agreed not to request any long-term foreign credits greater than the Anglo-American loan between 1945 and 1951. That left the waiver of payments problem: what would keep Britain from refusing to pay the United States interest in order to meet its debt obligations to other foreign countries? Dean Acheson addressed this concern to the American public, saying, "And remember this too: If interest payments on the loan are waived by the United States, then Great Britain must have her other creditors waive interest payments on *their* loans to her."[120] Since Britain had defaulted on its World War I debts, Clayton and Vinson took every precaution to ensure that this loan would indeed be, as Vinson argued, "not an expenditure but an investment."[121]

While there was no explicit requirement for how Britain would use the funds in the final agreement, it was understood that, as Dalton explained, "we should agree to use the assistance given to U.S. for progressive removal of discrimination and to secure writing down of sterling balances by voluntary agreement with each creditor."[122] Britain agreed to this requirement because it expected that it could negotiate its other foreign loans in order to avoid an excessive drawing on its dollar pool, but it was unable to do so. The United States had settled lend-lease at

---

[119] Hugh Dalton, "Washington Financial Talks," 2.
[120] Acheson, 9.
[121] "Vinson Campaigns for British Loan," *The New York Times*, January 9, 1946.
[122] Hugh Dalton, "Washington Financial Talks," 2.

only $650,000 at the time of the loan, and it was the hope that other countries would follow suit. However, other large lenders to Britain, like India and Egypt, were less economically developed and argued that it would not be feasible for them to maintain the same standards as the wealthy United States.

The American negotiators used the loan as the ultimate bargaining chip in the breakdown of Britain's trade barriers, an effort that Roosevelt had espoused since Imperial Preference's inception in 1932. The loan was the only means by which the United States could motivate Britain to dismantle this preference system, but it also ironically provided the financial support necessary for Britain to adopt the stipulations of the loan.[123] The Americans felt the agreement was not just a "tit-for-tat" arrangement, but rather, it assured financial security for both countries after the war. Britain felt differently, having given up its historical trade advantages for a $3.75 billion lifeline to avoid short-term default.

This inter-dependence between trade and the loan was furthered by the publication of the joint American and British statement on commercial policy alongside the loan agreements. As early as Dalton's November 1945 telegram, the loan was tied to British "support [for] the Americans in their proposals for an international conference as the preliminary to the setting up of an International Trade Organization."[124] Dean Acheson called this arrangement "the most important part of the agreement."[125] It was this preoccupation of both countries with international trade that caused the loan to go from a $5 billion credit proposal (no interest, no strings attached)

---

[123] Richard M. Freeland, *The Truman Doctrine and the Origins of McCarthyism: Foreign Policy, Domestic Politics, and Internal Security: 1946-1948* (New York: Alfred A. Knopf, 1972): 48. Freeland argues that the loan's "obligations amounted to substantial commitments to adopt multilateral policies in the face of highly uncertain economic circumstances in Britain."

[124] Hugh Dalton, "Washington Financial Talks," 2.

[125] Acheson, 7-8.

to a $3.75 billion loan (at 2% interest but with requirements of multilateralism, sterling-dollar convertibility, and participation in Bretton Woods).

On December 6, 1945, President Truman and Prime Minister Attlee issued a statement announcing the financial agreement, the Joint Statement on Commercial Policy, and the Joint Statement on Settlement for Lend-Lease and Reciprocal Aid, Surplus War Property, and Claims. The two declared that the loan would allow the United Kingdom "generally to move forward with the United States and other countries toward the common objective of expanded multilateral trade."[126] They posited the loan as a war deterrent, saying, "the arrangements, if carried out, will put an end to the fear of an economically divided world."[127] At the same time, Keynes and Halifax issued a statement of the agreement to Parliament from Washington, citing the purpose of the loan as to "assist the Government of the United Kingdom to assume the obligations of multilateral trade."[128] Despite this optimistic jargon, it was clear that the Americans had shamelessly utilized their superior financial position to push a specific international agenda alongside the loan. The loan's many stipulations were a brutal reminder of Britain's loss of international dominance. Insult was added to injury when Keynes and Halifax were sent to secure Parliament's approval of the loan and its requirements before the United States Congress would even consider approving its funding.

## Chapter Three: British Parliamentary Debates

---

[126] "Anglo-American Financial and Commercial Agreements," The U.S. Department of State, December 1945, http://fraser.stlouisfed.org/docs/historical/martin/17_07_19451206.pdf.

[127] "Anglo-American Financial and Commercial Agreements," The U.S. Department of State.

[128] John Maynard Keynes and Lord Halifax, "Financial Agreement Between His Majesty's Government in the United Kingdom and the Government of the United States," (London: His Majesty's Stationary Office, December 6, 1945).

Keynes and Halifax returned to London downtrodden. After boasting to his colleagues that he could easily obtain a sizeable grant from the United States, Keynes came back with much less. According to one reporter, Keynes "returned to London by air [on December 17, 1945] just a few hours before he rose in the small, crowded chamber where the Lords meet, looking so wan and gray that one of his peers murmured: 'He's killing himself in this business.'"[129] In his statement, Keynes detailed the fierce nature of his meetings abroad and highlighted American resentment of the loan. He explained the proposal's transformation from a grant to a loan, saying, "nothing else was possible in the complex and highly charged atmosphere of that great democracy."[130] Still, Keynes and Halifax claimed small but significant successes in their insistence on interest payment waivers, a low interest rate, and a transition period for international convertibility and the end of imperial preference. The negotiations were no small feat. Chancellor of the Exchequer Hugh Dalton even wrote to Keynes, "Thank you from the bottom of my heart for all you have accomplished…you have got us the dollars, without which— though I have more than once thought that a break might have to come—the near future would have been black as a pit! I am very deeply grateful to you, and so are my colleagues. Even those who least liked some details of the Agreement are loud in praise of your skill, resource, and patience."[131] Dalton sympathized with Keynes, downplaying the resentment many British politicians and citizens felt towards the loan proposal. Instead, Keynes met a hostile reception in Parliament because of the hype leading up to the grant and British shock at their ally's lack of

---

[129] Anne O'Hare McCormick, " 'Underlying Realities' in the Debate on the British Loan," *The New York Times,* April 24, 1946. http://query.nytimes.com/mem/archive/pdf?res=F10717FD385E1B7B93C6AB178FD85F428485F9. Keynes passed away on April 21, 1946 of a heart attack, after being "exhausted by the strain of the International Monetary Conference at Savannah, G.A.," according to his obituary in *The New York Times.* See: www.nytimes.com/learning/general/onthisday/bday/0605.html.

[130] John Maynard Keynes, quoted by McCormick, "Underlying Realities."

[131] Hugh Dalton to John Maynard Keynes, December 5, 1945. *The Collected Writings of John Maynard Keynes,* volume 24, edited by Donald Moggridge, (Cambridge and London: Cambridge University Press, 1971-1989): 604.

generosity.

Figure 15: "Don't touch it, they're only after the salvage"
Britain is sinking. Harry Truman and George Marshall cast a rope out to him spelling "Maid,"
since they are cleaning up Britain's mess. A man marked "the Critics" (of the loan and American
aid) cries, "Don't touch it, they're only after the salvage."
Leslie Gillbert Illingworth, *The Daily Mail* (London), July 17, 1948.
The National Library of Wales.

In general, Conservatives were opposed to the loan and Labour supported it. Most Conservatives rejected the negotiations because of their insult to British authority and the threat to the British hold over the colonies. Labour politicians needed the money to finance their domestic policies, but they were wary of the unpopular dismantling of imperial preference. Likewise, the British public and press were largely split along political lines in their reactions to the negotiations. The Tory imperialist *Daily Mail* advocated ending the negotiations after news of the American counter-proposals, whereas the Labour-affiliated *Daily Herald* supported Labour's fierce negotiating team.[132] However, this simple dichotomy underestimates the complexity of the loan debates. Surprisingly, notable leaders like Winston Churchill and Clement Attlee were comparatively silent on the issue in comparison to their subordinates. This could be explained as a strategic ploy to stay above the political fray. Instead, their leadership was more behind the scenes.

Attlee and his officials exerted great pressure on Parliament to consolidate support for the loan. The Labour party refused to be responsible for extending the economic depression as their predecessors had done in the interwar period. Hugh Dalton connected the loan's passage to Labour's promise of full employment in particular, saying in his November loan proposal that "this acceptance would be accompanied by an interpretive declaration that nothing in the Final Act would require us to adopt an internal deflationary policy at a time of unemployment."[133] The loan seemed to guarantee a future for Labour's campaign promises.

Some Labour politicians opposed the loan. Labour leader Hugh Gaitskell critiqued the lack of clarity in the loan's stipulations, saying "how far, then, we shall eventually travel along the road to complete multilateralism and non-discrimination depends partly on the outcome of

---

[132] Peter Clarke, *The Last Thousand Days*, 378.
[133] Hugh Dalton, "Washington Financial Talks,"2.

the trade conference [scheduled for fall 1947] and partly on the way in which the present and future agreements are interpreted."[134] In essence, Britain had relinquished control over its monetary and economic policies to an international organization that could interpret the loan requirements as it wished. The loan's lack of clarity meant that its effects were indeterminable at the time of its passage. Gaitskell termed the loan "nasty but necessary," since the implementation of its stipulations would inspire international debates long past its passage.[135]

Criticism of the loan was particularly sharp among conspicuous leftists in the Labour Party, like Aneurin Bevan and Emanuel Shinwell, who argued that the loan was insulting and avoidable. Bevan, the Labour Minister of Health who spearheaded the creation of the National Health Service, was concerned by American efforts to dictate Britain's economic policies. He even compared the loan to the Combination Acts of 1799 and 1800, which stripped workers of their rights by outlawing labor unions and collective bargaining. Like these laws, he argued, the financial agreement "in the sacred name of free competition, purported to impose the same rules on masters and men."[136] The loan required that England and its colonies trade on the same multilateral terms. Without the protection of Great Britain, the colonies would suffer economically and be unable to compete with economic giants like the United States. In addition, Bevan argued that the loan negotiations could have been strategically paused to garner more support from British citizens rather than hurriedly accepted under such disadvantageous conditions.[137] He accused the negotiators of the loan of allowing their desperation to cloud their judgment.

---

[134] Hugh Gaitskell was Minister of Fuel and Power from 1947-1950, succeeded Stafford Cripps as Chancellor of the Exchequer from 1950-1951, and led the Labour Party as Leader of the Opposition from 1955-1963. Hugh Gaitskell, "More about the Loan," *The Spectator* (January 18, 1946), 8, http://archive.spectator.co.uk/article/18th-january-1946/8/more-about-the-loan.

[135] Hugh Gaitskell, "More about the Loan."

[136] Michael Foot, *Aneurin Bevan: A Biography, Volume 2: 1945-1960* (London: Faber and Faber, 2009), 57.

[137] Foot, 57.

HERE HE COMES, BOYS !

Figure 16: Aneurin Bevan faced substantial criticism for his work on the National Health Insurance Act, which passed in 1946 and created a state health service for all British citizens. Harley Street in London was well-known for housing many wealthy doctors. Victor Weisz, *News Chronicle* (London), August 7, 1945.[138]

Fellow progressive Emanuel (Manny) Shinwell, who served as Minister of Fuel and Power from 1945-1947 and then as Secretary of State for War and Minister of Defense, joined Bevan in denouncing the loan. Shinwell was a well-known member of the "Red Clydesides," a Scottish radical interest group that began with workers' opposition to World War I. It supported multiple labor strikes between 1911 and 1920, but remained a politically active as an extremely leftist wing of the Labour party.[139] In particular, Shinwell argued that the loan was not only

---

[138] Victor Weisz (Vicky) was a German freelance cartoonist who worked for the magazine *12 Uhr Blatt*. As a Jews, his cartoons were firmly anti-Hitler. When the magazine was taken over by Nazis in 1933, Blatt left for Britain and worked for the *Evening Standard, News Chronicle, New Statesman, Daily Mail,* and *Daily Mirror.* He was a prominent Left-wing cartoonist. *News Chronicle* ended publication in 1960, when it was absorbed by *The Daily Mail.*

[139] The Red Clydesides helped organize a 1911 strike of 11,000 workers at Singer sewings machine factory

unnecessary for the Labour agenda, but it would also their goals. It was hypocritical to adopt American free trade policies under the loan while implementing Labour's proposed planned economy.[140] The *laissez-faire* stipulations were in direct contrast with Labour's advocacy of government intervention as the best way to maintain a strong economy. Both Shinwell and Bevan advocated a rejection of the loan to protect British autonomy.

The loan's requirement for interest payments united Labourites and Conservatives, as well as supporters and critics alike in resentment towards the United States. It seemed absurd to add to British debt, especially when the Americans demanded that the loan could not be used to repay the country's existing sterling obligations. Financing additional debt would be even more difficult if their economy suffered under new free trade policies as expected. Conservative Robert Boothby, who had formerly served as Churchill's private secretary, analyzed the country's mounting debt obligations, estimating to Parliament that "annual payments for [the loan's] interest and amortization of our sterling obligations, if paid in full on the basis of two per cent, amount to about 70 million pounds a year…[all] under conditions of free currency convertibility, unplanned promiscuous trade, and cut throat competition."[141] Surprisingly, Keynes himself shared this concern, and openly admitted his own concern with the loan's terms, declaring to Parliament, "on the matter of interest, I shall never so long as I live cease to regret that this is not an interest-free loan. The charging of interest is out of tune with the under-lying

---

in Clydebank, a 1915 strike against rent increases, and the "40 hour strike" of 1919, which rallied trade unions in Glasgow, Scotland for a 40-hour work week. They also protested Britain's involvement in World War I. Manny Shinwell grew up in Glasgow, where at a young age he became involved in the Amalgated Union of Clothing Operatives, British Seafarers' Union, Amalgated Marine Workers' Union, National Sailors' and Firemans' Union, and the Glasgow 40 Hours Movement. After serving as a Labour MP (with a few losses) since 1922, Shinwell became Chairman of the Labour Party in 1942. Later serving as Minister of Fuel and Power, he oversaw the nationalization of the coal and mining industries and had to deal with criticism during Britain's coal shortage in the winter of 1947.

[140] Richard Toye, *The Labour Party and the Planned Economy, 1931-1951*, (London: Boydell Press for the Royal Historical Society, 2003), 156.

[141] Robert Boothby, "Anglo-American Loan Agreement," (Speech, London, The House of Commons, July 19, 1946), vol. 425 cc1611-46, http://hansard.millbanksystems.com/commons/1946/jul/19/anglo-american-loan-agreement#S5CV0425P0_19460719_HOC_130.

realities."[142] This inclusion of two percent interest, even on favorable terms like the 50-year repayment period, seemed to most British politicians to be an unnecessary final slight by the Americans. The interest amount was negligible to the United States but extraordinary to Britain.

Figure 16: "Britannia and the U.S. Loan"
Conservative Parliamentarians Lord Beaverbrook and Robert Boothby prevent Britannia, who is loaded with "Britain Post War Burdens," from joining President Harry Truman, Secretary of State James Byrnes, and Keynes in a car labeled "U.S Loan."
Leslie Gilbert Illingworth, *The Daily Mail* (London), December 10, 1945.
The National Library of Wales.

Keynes and Halifax blamed Clayton and Vinson for insisting so vigorously that interest be charged, insulting their ability to harness support from their colleagues. Keynes explained, "It is precisely in our agreeing to at least the appearance of interest that the Americans are adamant. For my part, I am not persuaded that bold leadership could not put through an interest free loan."[143] Likewise, Halifax wrote to Churchill that:

---

[142] John Maynard Keynes, "Anglo-American Financial Agreements," December 18, 1945, Vol. 138, No. 41, King's College Cambridge, J.M.K. Papers.
[143] John Maynard Keynes, Letter to Mr. Governor Catto, October 22, 1945, King's College Cambridge, J.M.K. Papers.

The trouble has been that they imagined, and having imagined magnified, their own political difficulties to a greater extent than I believe a more courageous leadership would have accepted and they could I believe by taking perhaps a slightly greater risk with their public opinion have got away with something that would have smelled very much sweeter on the British side and proved itself in the long run a very much larger act of statesmanship than what they have in fact achieved.[144]

The Americans' pretext that their public needed to believe that the loan was a good investment garnered further anger from their British counterparts, since they too had to gain public support for the loan.

Still, most Labour politicians bitterly accepted the loan as medicine for their diseased economy. The loan would support the country's domestic economy in the short term as Attlee and his administration fulfilled their campaign promises. On the other hand, Conservative politicians turned their focus to international policies, sustaining substantial concerns with the loan's requirement that Britain adopt multilateral trade policies. Robert Boothby, an MP who had previously served as Churchill's parliamentary secretary, proclaimed that, "When we are all waving our hats in the air about American films and Virginian cigarettes, and that little bit of extra petrol, I think we ought constantly to bear in mind the situation which will confront us one year hence, when we take the first plunge into the icy sea of free convertibility and multilateral free trade."[145] The dangers of abandoning protectionist measures were extremely apparent. Many Conservatives considered any policies that would weaken the British colonial stronghold unacceptable, especially as India and Pakistan became increasingly restless.[146]

Conservatives also objected to the loan's role in financing Britain's purchase of exports

NOV. 10

FIFTH AVENUE CIGARETTES

Specially prepared by Abdulla for all lovers
of the American style cigarette

FIFTH AVENUE        20 for 2/4
173 New Bond St., W.1.

---

[144] Lord Halifax, Letter to Winston, December 3, 194[  ] Cambridge.
[145] Hansard Parliamentary Debates, House of Comm[  ]
http://hansard.millbanksystems.com/commons/1946/jul/19/an[  ]
[146] Both became independent countries the year after[  ]

from the United States. In many ways, Britain was actually doing the United States a favor by accepting the loan. The loan ensured England and its colonies would be a customer for the enormous manufacturing capacity America developed during wartime. Even British politicians who supported the agreement recognized this. Labour Chancellor Dalton did not even attempt to counter complaints that the loan was being used to buy U.S. films rather than more essential items like food, responding simply, "British people like United States films."[147] He and other loan supporters had resigned themselves to the reality that American imports were in demand and the loan would help end austerity. Many conservatives, however, argued that spending the credit to support American rather than British industries was insulting and absurd.

Figure 17: "American-style cigarettes" advertisement, *The Daily Mail*, October 24, 1945
Hugh Dalton Archives, London School of Economics

As a result, it seemed likely that most Conservatives would vote against the loan, impeding its passage in Parliament. These critics were led by Leopold Amery, a politician who served as Secretary of State for India and Burma from 1940-1945 and was perhaps the most vocal opponent of the loan.[148] Amery authored *The Washington Loan Agreements: A Critical Study of American Economic Foreign Policy* in 1946, which detailed his extreme dissatisfaction with the loan proposal.[149] Amery argued that sterling-dollar convertibility would result in a "return to the unplanned world economy of the nineteenth century and to the limitations of the

---

[147] Hugh Dalton, "Anglo-American Loan (U.S. Films)," (House of Commons Debates, October 15, 1946), vol. 427 c151W, http://hansard.millbanksystems.com/written_answers/1946/oct/15/anglo-american-loan-us-films#S5CV0427P0_19461015_CWA_21.

[148] Amery had previously opposed the League of Nations, arguing that the world is not equal so each country should not be treated on an equal basis. Likewise, he opposed appeasement with Germany on the eve of World War II. See also: Leopold Amery, *The Fundamental Fallacies of Free Trade* (London: National Review Office, 1908) https://archive.org/stream/fundamentalfalla00ameruoft#page/n5/mode/2up.

[149] Leopold Amery, *The Washington Loan Agreements: A Critical Study of American Economic Foreign Policy* (London: Macdonald & Co. Publishers, 1946).

gold standard."[150] Other conservative Parliamentarians agreed, even quoting Winthrop Aldrich, American President of Chase Bank, as saying that Bretton Woods is a "further application of the Gold Standard." [151] Sterling convertibility meant that the nation had to relinquish control over its currency to the market. During the Great Depression, the United States had forced citizens and Federal Reserve Banks to sell all gold to the Treasury, outlawed private gold ownership, and effectively abandoned the gold standard.[152] The U.S. government also committed to converting dollars into gold at $35 per ounce for foreign governments and central banks to bolster faith in the dollar as a new reserve currency. Thus, international convertibility meant adopting a de facto gold standard. The American economy would have an unprecedented amount of influence over British monetary policy. Amery was so concerned about potential deference to American economic leadership that he called for a "British Declaration of Independence," a phrase that later titled fellow Conservative politician Henry Drummond-Wolff's 1948 book, which promoted increased economic interdependence within the British Empire rather than American multilateralism.[153] Amery and Drummond-Wolff argued that the loan threatened the key to Britain's economic prowess: the Sterling Area.

This intense fear of the gold standard was a response to recent history. After World War I, the U.S. and many other governments retained wartime measures that abandoned the gold standard.[154] Britain returned to the pre-war gold standard to promote its financial strength and foster international confidence in the pound sterling, while all other countries retained their

---

[150] E.C. Franklin, "Sterling System v. Bretton Woods and U.S. Loan," *Auckland Star*, February 7, 1946.

[151] Richard Stokes, "Anglo-American Financial and Economic Discussions," (House of Commons Debates, December 13, 1945), vol. 417 cc641-739, http://hansard.millbanksystems.com/commons/1945/dec/13/anglo-american-financial-and-economic.

[152] The President also devalued the dollar from $20.67 per gold ounce to $35 per gold ounce.

[153] Inderjeet Parmar, *Special Interests, the State and the Anglo-American Alliance, 1939-1945* (London and Portland, Oregon: Frank Cass, 1995), 171. Henry-Drummond Wolff, *British Declaration of Independence* (London and New York: Hutchinson, 1948).

[154] In the United States, this policy was formalized with the 1933 laws forbidding private gold ownership and consolidation of gold reserves in the U.S. Treasury.

wartime convertibility.[155] This restriction led to overvaluation of the sterling, dramatically increasing the cost of British exports, causing high interest rates, and decreasing employment. This made borrowing money more difficult for both the nation as a whole and for the individual citizen, deepening the economic depression. In addition, maintenance of the gold standard necessitated loans from France and the United States, which had large gold reserves.

Thus, in an effort to implement austerity policies, the existing Labour government was forced to default on its campaign promises.[156] The second Labour administration in British history had been elected in 1929 based on candidate Ramsay MacDonald's campaign promises of public housing and national healthcare. The United States had offered loans to support Britain's gold standard policies, but domestic troubles from the Great Depression obliged Congress to tighten its purse strings. In August 1931, U.S. President Herbert Hoover told Secretary of State Henry Stimson the United States could no longer lend to Britain because of domestic economic concerns.[157] Within weeks, intense pressure caused Prime Minister MacDonald to resign. The national unity coalition that formed the new government immediately abandoned the gold standard, allowing for increased exports and lifting the country out of recession. The Labour party was left with an infamous legacy for poor financial leadership. The country came away from the crisis with a profound distaste for the gold standard.[158] The Attlee Administration's own lack of substantial economic planning brought back memories of the difficult interwar period, and as a result, both Labour and Conservative politicians feared any association with the gold standard.

---

[155] Britain returned to the gold standard in 1925.
[156] National Archives Exhibitions, "First World War,"
http://www.nationalarchives.gov.uk/pathways/firstworldwar/aftermath/brit_after_war.htm.
[157] Brian J.C. MacKercher, *Transition of Power*, (Cambridge University Press, 1990), 93.
[158] MacKercher, 93.

Amery invoked these concerns of the gold standard in his *The Washington Loan Agreements*. He claimed that convertibility would not only cause the same economic problems that occurred in the 1930s, but it would also destabilize what had been the solution to the Great Depression: the development of the Sterling Area and close trade ties between the colonies.[159] Convertibility was an offense to the entire British Empire, and prominent economist Roy Harrod summarized Amery's view of the loan as "mainly designed to break up the Empire."[160] Acceptance of this "retrograde policy" meant risking another economic downturn, as well as diminished political influence over the colonies.[161]

In addition, Amery criticized Labour negotiators for not standing up against the "tough guys" of Congress, accusing the British government of "defeatism."[162] Amery may have held a grudge after having lost his Parliamentary seat to Labour just months before, but it is also true that Attlee's administration had been unable to realize both its campaign promises of social welfare and implement the necessary post-war austerity measures. Historian Fred Block later agreed with Amery, writing "it was both economic and political timidity that led the Labour government to follow Lord Keynes down the path of American-inspired multilateralism."[163] Amery argued that nationalist capitalism with a preference for the Sterling Area was a viable alternative to accepting an American-imposed multilateralism. He also warned that Britain would be unprotected if a trade war broke out between the U.S. and Soviet governments. He claimed that economic warfare would not stem from continued protectionist measures but rather from

---

[159] After the new government removed the gold standard and devalued the sterling in September 1931, many countries followed suit and instead pegged their currencies to sterling. These countries kept their reserves at the Bank of England, which instituted strict exchange controls to protect the external value of sterling. Member countries could trade freely amongst themselves, and they had guaranteed access to the London financial markets. The British government could in turn rely on the entire area's reserves to support the value of sterling.

[160] Roy F. Harrod. "Review of *The Washington Loan Agreements*," 88.

[161] Amery, *The Washington loan* Agreements, v.

[162] Franklin, "Sterling System v. Bretton Woods and U.S. Loan."

[163] Block, 64.

Soviet and American attempts to "pursue aggressive economic policies and to force them on other countries."[164] If she was not careful, Britain could be a victim of Soviet-American competition.

Amery's disgust for the loan was well-publicized in the British press. He was considered an expert on India, having been born there while his father was an officer in the Indian Forestry Commission. Amery learned Hindi as a child, and served as First Lord of the Admiralty and Secretary of State for the Colonies in the interwar period before becoming Secretary of State for India and Burma in 1940. Because India was Britain's largest creditor of the colonies, he had a particular interest in the post-war debt plans.[165]

Unlike Amery, former Prime Minister Winston Churchill strongly supported the loan, despite his Conservative allegiance. Churchill had been shocked that Truman ended Lend-Lease so suddenly and "proceed[ed] in such a rough and harsh manner as to hamper a faithful ally." [166] He placed great faith in the Anglo-American partnership, so even after his election defeat, the former Prime Minister supported the Labour government in its attempts to maintain a strong relationship with the United States. Churchill was notably quiet in the Parliament debates regarding his support for the loan, preferring to convince his colleagues in private. In fact, Churchill's main public role was his promotion of the loan to Americans, not to the British during a March 1946 trip to the States, long after the British Parliamentary debates had been decided.[167] According to Keynes, Churchill "told all his friends that he was in favour of the loan, that we needed it, and that the argument against lending to a Socialist Government was a wrong

---

[164] Franklin, "Sterling System v. Bretton Woods and U.S. Loan."
[165] Clarke, *The Last Thousand Days*, 383.
[166] Clarke, *The Last Thousand Days*, 374.
[167] The British Parliament had already agreed to the loan's conditions in December 1945, so the trip only influenced whether the U.S. Congress approved its funding.

and invalid argument, with which we would have nothing to do."[168] Like Keynes, Churchill saw

a renewed Anglo-American alliance as key to establishing a balance of power after the war.

Amery and Churchill were in fact close friends and classmates from the Harrow School,

one of Britain's leading all-male boarding schools. During Amery's time as a war correspondent

for *The Times* during the Boer War, he and Churchill narrowly escaped captivity together. Still,

Churchill and Avery disagreed about India's post-war fate. Churchill wanted it to remain

completely submissive to Britain, while Amery saw an opportunity for the Dominions to

gradually evolve into strong, independent nations that would still remain intensely loyal to

Britain through strong trade preferences and economic integration. For Amery, imperial

economic integration was more essential than political alliance, while Churchill saw the two as

indivisible.

Churchill and Amery also had conflicting opinions of free trade. During the 1906 general

election, Amery published "The Fallacies of Free Trade," in which he attacked Adam Smith's

*The Wealth of Nations* (1776) and its promotion of the free market's "invisible hand." Amery

argued that *lassiez-faire* policies foolishly assume that people act without regard to their

"community whether large or small."[169] He claimed that while the individual may know his

interests best under a certain set of circumstances, federal economic policies help alter those

circumstances for the better.[170] Amery also published articles in *The Times* arguing against free

trade under the penname "Tariff Reformer." That same year, Churchill wrote the political

pamphlet *For Free Trade*. He campaigned for the traditionally Tory Manchester North-West as a

Liberal and won in part because Tories were split on the trade issue.[171] The pamphlet included

---

[168] John Maynard Keynes, *The Collected Writings of John Maynard Keynes*, volume 27, edited by Donald Moggridge, (Cambridge and London: Cambridge University Press, 1971-1989): 482-483 as quoted in Clarke, 423.
[169] Amery, *The Fundamental Fallacies of Free Trade*, 7.
[170] Amery, *The Fundamental Fallacies of Trade*, 12-13.
[171] Winston S. Churchill, *For Free Trade*, (1906; London: Churchilliana Co, 1977 reprint)

his numerous speeches against the tariffs and other protectionist trade policies. In one speech he argued: "Will the shutting out of foreign goods increase the total amount of wealth in this country? Can foreign nations grow rich at our expense by selling U.S. goods under cost price? Can a people tax themselves into prosperity? Can a man stand in a bucket and lift himself up by the handle?"[172] This debate continued after World War II and reveals why Churchill ended up supporting the loan and Amery did not.

Both men strongly supported the Empire at all costs. Amery appealed to Churchill's concern for imperialism in his anti-loan manifesto, declaring, "No more than Mr. Churchill am I prepared to acquiesce in the liquidation and breakup of the British Empire."[173] Amery considered the loan's free trade stipulations a direct offense to his convictions regarding Indian-British relations. He wrote, "the British Empire is the oyster which this loan is prise to open. Each part of it, deprived of the mutual support of the Empire Preference, is to be swallowed separately, to become a field for American industrial exploitation, a tributary of American finance, and, in the end, an American dependency."[174] This is where the two Conservatives' views of the loan diverged. Churchill was quoted as saying, "I cannot see that there is the slightest justification for suggesting that we are compromised and fettered in any way in respect of Imperial preference."[175] He had much more faith in American generosity. It is true that Churchill had a strong preoccupation with the strength of the Empire, but he also had an additional priority that Amery discounted – the 'special' Anglo-American relationship.

---

http://www.churchillbooks.com/GuidePDFs/g8.pdf
[172] Winston S. Churchill, "Speech at the Free Trade Hall" (1904), Manchester England, *For Free Trade* (1906; London: Churchilliana Co, 1977 reprint).
[173] Amery, *The Washington Loan Agreements*, xi.
[174] Amery, *The Washington Loan Agreements*, xi.
[175] Lord Pakenham, "Anglo-American Financial Arrangements," December 17, 1945. Hansard Parliamentary Debates, House of Lords, vol 138 cc677-776.

This steadfast belief in Anglo-American cooperation defined Churchill's opinion of the loan. Not only had he worked during the war as Prime Minister to promote the alliance, but he was also half-American. Churchill considered the partnership as essential for British success in the post-war era, and borrowing from the United States could only help strengthen that bond. He believed that the alliance would ensure continued British world influence rather than diminish it. Despite his concerns with potential threats to the Empire, this support for Anglo-American partnership combined with his conviction in free trade made voting against the loan unacceptable. While he supported the loan, Churchill still recognized how politically unpopular it was. He advocated abstention, saying, "I cannot understand why we—the Opposition, the minority—should be expected to come forward to approve and welcome a proposal which fills every party in the House with great anxiety, and which is only commended to us by the fear of an even darker alternative. It is for the Government and their great majority to bear the burden.[176]" This convinced many Conservatives to join him in abstaining from the vote, preventing it from sure defeat.

The most divisive issue for both supporters and opponents of the loan was the question of the Americans' motives. Keynes tried to understand the justification for the loan's conditions. Keynes told Parliament:

> For after living here [in Washington] some weeks, one cannot doubt the genuine difficulties with which Vinson and Clayton will be faced when they try to sell the settlement to Congress. During the whole of my visit here there has not been a single major proposal that he President has put to Congress that Congress has accepted. Once we have come to terms with Vinson and Clayton they will have to fight on our behalf like tigers if they are to have any hope of victory.[177]

---

[176] Winston S. Churchill, "Anglo-American Financial and Economic Discussions," Hansard Parliamentary Debates, vol 417 cc641-739, House of Commons, December 13, 1945, http://hansard.millbanksystems.com/commons/1945/dec/13/anglo-american-financial-and-economic.

[177] John Maynard Keynes, Letter to Mr. Governor Catto, October 22, 1945, King's College Cambridge, J.M.K. Papers. Thomas Silveright Catto, 1st Baron Catto was the Governor of the Bank of England from 1944 to 1949, and helped oversee its nationalization in 1946.

American domestic politics were considered a hard limit for British interests. Conservatives

Boothby and Amery disagreed. They saw the Americans as selfish and ruthless, using their need

to sell the deal to Congress as an excuse to play hardball with the British.[178] Conservative

member Frederick Marquis, also known as Lord Woolton, criticized Keynes's previous warning

of a "financial Dunkirk" without a loan, arguing that the loan itself would actually be a Dunkirk

because "we are surrendering to the power of the dollar."[179] America "had become rich beyond

her dreams" from the war, and yet England still had to relinquish her pride to gain limited

assistance with extraordinary stipulations, amounting to an unforgivable insult. [180] These

arguments agree with not only Conservative Leopold Amery's stance, but they also reflect

extreme Labour members Emanuel Shinwell and Aneurin Bevan's statements that the loan was

unnecessary and avoidable. Still, Woolton, the current Conservative Party chairman, joined

Amery in considering these negotiations a testament to the Labour Party's inexperience and

inaptitude. Later, Woolton channeled this resentment into the 1951 election, where he secured a

Conservative victory by painting the Labour Party as Soviet-friendly Socialists. Woolton shifted

the conversation from blaming the American Congress to the British domestic government. The

economic arguments surrounding the loan had become political foundations to condemn the

current administration.

Anglo-Canadian business tycoon and Conservative politician Lord Beaverbrook was also

concerned about the loan's conditions. After serving in the coalition government as Minister of

---

[178] This is evidenced in the discussion of the interest rate. Clayton and Vinson argued that it was necessary for the aid to be in the form of a loan, not a grant, since it would be an easier sell to the American public. The idea of the loan as a business investment was publicized in U.S. State Department promotion materials and in Truman and Attlee's statements on December 6, 1945 after Parliament passed the loan.

[179] "Lords' Loan Opposition More Vocal Than Voting," *Australian Associated Press*, December 19, 1945, 2 http://trove.nla.gov.au/ndp/del/article/26141061.

[180] Benn Steil, *The Battle of Bretton Woods: John Maynard Keynes, Harry Dexter White, and the Making of a New Order* (Princeton University Press, 2013), 285.

Aircraft Production, Supply and War Production, he was appointed Lord Privy Seal before retiring from politics in 1945. Beaverbrook became a press mogul, acquiring *The Daily Express, London Evening Standard*, and the *Sunday Evening Express*. Still, he remained involved in politics and participated in House of Lords' debates on the loan. He joined his fellow Conservatives in arguing that the agreement was a thinly veiled threat to British hold over the colonies. Having been born in Canada and founded the Calgary Power Company, Beaverbrook had a unique perspective on England's relationship with her colonies.[181] Like Amery, Beaverbrook considered economic integration vital to the dominions' financial success.

Figure 18: Beaverbrook was strongly opposed to any threat to trade within the Empire.

---

[181] The Calgary Power Company is now TransAlta Corporation, and was founded in 1909. Many Canadian homes were lit for the first time by Calgary Power because residential power was just becoming widespread. TransAlta is currently Canada's largest publicly traded energy generator.

Sidney George Strube, *Daily Express* (London), September 21, 1945.[182]
Leopold Amery Archives, Churchill College Archive Centre, Cambridge University.

However, unlike his colleagues, Beaverbrook was sympathetic to American reasons for introducing the loan's stipulations, even calling them "altruistic motives."[183] He claimed that the loan was avoidable because American goods could be substituted with goods from within the Empire – such as foodstuffs from Holland, Denmark, and Belgium; cotton from Britain's own reserves; tobacco from Canada, Rhodesia, and the Balkan States; and oil from Persia. Britain could use its status as the largest market for the United States as a bargaining chip to retain its economic independence rather than an obligation. Beaverbrook also spoke for the Dominions, arguing that fears of their potential default to the dollar from the Sterling Area were unfounded. Preexisting economic integration would guarantee a long-term alliance, Beaverbrook argued, even if sterling-based currencies were threatened. For example, England imported two-thirds of Canada's agricultural exports. He warned Parliamentarians not to discount the power of imperial sentiment, especially since "Canada has announced her intention of helping us in a very big way."[184] Accepting the financial agreement would strengthen relations with the United States, but it would also weaken ties with the Dominions. Beaverbrook felt that the potential downfalls outweighed any benefits of the loan.

The American public was kept fully informed of Britain's reluctance to accept their loan stipulations. "Any American who imagines that it is easier to receive than to give aid should see how the ordinary Britisher dislikes the necessity of accepting conditions which seem to him

---

[182] George Strube worked for the *Daily Express*, becoming one of the highest paid cartoonists of his time, earning 10,000 pounds a year in 1931. He married prominent *Daily Express* fashion artist Marie Allwright.

[183] Lord Beaverbrook, "Anglo-American Financial Arrangements," (Speech, London, The House of Lords, December 18, 1945), vol. 138 c777-897, http://hansard.millbanksystems.com/lords/1945/dec/18/anglo-american-financial-arrangements#S5LV0138P0_19451218_HOL_102.

[184] Lord Beaverbrook, "Anglo-American Financial Arrangements."

galling and fettering," one *The New York Times* columnist explained.[185] Neither country was under the illusion that this loan was a generous gift, no matter how hard the negotiators attempted to portray it as such. The *New York Times* author bluntly stated: "The British resent the terms because they limit British freedom and give U.S. the upper hand."[186] This was a power struggle, and the Americans were winning.

The Truman administration refused to fully admit the manipulative nature of the stipulations added to the loan. When asked why a quid pro quo approach, whereby Britain would give the United States naval bases in order to receive funds, was not considered, Dean Acheson asserted that "to demand such concessions as part of the loan agreement would have been like saying to Britain, 'Sure we'll help you get back on your feet, but not unless you hand over some of your territory, and do things our way from now on.' You can imagine how any self-respecting nation would react to that."[187] This seemed absurd to the British who felt the loan stipulations were exactly such an offensive concession. By signing the agreement, Britain would effectively be agreeing to "do things…[the American] way from now on."[188] As the Duke of Bedford, a member of the House of Lords, claimed before Parliament, "We are proposing to hand over the control of our economic life, in a very large measure, to a gang of representatives of Wall street finance who are responsible to no one and are above every government."[189] This loss of autonomy deeply wounded the British, who felt undermined by their former ally.

In the end, Parliament reluctantly approved the loan on December 13, 1945, only 5 days after Truman and Attlee announced the proposal. The vote came to 345 ayes and 98 noes,

---

[185] McCormick, "British Loan as Precedent for Others."
[186] McCormick, "British Loan as Precedent for Others."
[187] Acheson, 12.
[188] Acheson, 12.
[189] Duke of Bedford, Hansard, House of Lords. As quoted by Vinson, U.S. Congress Committee on Banking and Currency, Anglo-American Financial Agreement Hearings, 79th Congress, 2nd Session, 1946, 19.

leaving 159 abstentions. Labour MPs followed Attlee in voting for the loan and for Bretton Woods, while almost all Conservative members led by Churchill, abstained.[190] This split along party lines did not reflect the diversity of opinion among British politicians and how controversial the loan had really become.[191] Instead, the divide reveals only the nominal allegiances of many politicians, not their true feelings regarding the loan and its conditions. The loan was also only debated for five days, which may explain the voters' default to party allegiance. Many politicians were angry about the hurried pace of debate and voting. Conservative Robert Boothby would later accuse Chancellor of the Exchequer Dalton of disrespecting Parliament's power, saying, "he has certainly brushed us aside from start to finish. He denied us the promised opportunity to discuss the Bretton Woods Agreement; and for the Loan Agreement we were allowed four days to do what it has now taken the Congress of the United States of America seven months to do."[192] Not only was Britain forced to accept the stipulations attached to the loan before Congress would even consider funding it, but it had done so in a desperate rush.

Previous historians have attributed the loan debate to partisan politics and its passage to economic desperation, without considering the wide variety of arguments present among both the loan's supporters and opponents. Each concern with the agreement offers insight into national anxieties present at the end of the war and deepens our understanding of the complex dynamics at play. The distaste for paying interest reveals British politicians' wounded ego and shock at the Americans' power politics, which extends across different party lines. Convertibility

---

[190] Conservative members held 197 seats, Labour had 393, and Liberals had 12 seats at the time. For a complete list of the votes, see: "Anglo-American Financial and Economic Discussions," Hansard Parliamentary Debates vol 417 cc641-739, House of Commons, December 13, 1945, http://hansard.millbanksystems.com/commons/1945/dec/13/anglo-american-financial-and-economic.

[191] The loan passed with a 247 majority and Bretton Woods passed with 314 votes for and 50 against.

[192] Robert Boothby, "Anglo-American Loan Agreement."

resurrected fears of an incapable Labour government, which was beginning to look more and more familiar. Lowering imperial preference and ending the Sterling Area seemed like American efforts to strip Britain of its political influence. In all, the loan negotiations made apparent Britain's attempts at self-preservation, and the inherent conflicts of those policies. The loan was necessary to save the country from financial default, but its conditions could threaten the very foundations of Britain's political and economic autonomy.

Chapter Four: American Congressional Approval

After passing in Parliament on December 6, 1945, the loan still had to be sold to a skeptical American public. Its funding was debated for almost seven months before narrow passage by Congress. The British foreign news correspondent for *The New York Times* noted the remarkable similarity of American and British debates over the loan, which both countries considered a "disagreeable necessity."[193] While the British opponents assumed that American politicians were united in enforcing the loan and its conditions, there was actually considerable debate over whether it would benefit the United States and its foreign policy.

Immediately after Parliament's approval of the loan, the Truman administration began selling it to Congress and the American public. Within days, Truman sent a special message to Congress about the financial agreement. He insisted that the loan was crucial to global trade and peace. He painted a scenario of economic warfare if the loan was not passed, saying, "if peace is to be permanent, we must never relax our efforts to make it so."[194] Secretary of State James Byrnes emphasized the same points as Truman at a dinner of the Foreign Policy Association in New York on February 11, 1946. He explained that the primary motivations for the loan were Britain's immediate financial needs, the dropping of barriers, and trade expansion.[195] These arguments were consistent with the priorities of Clayton and Vinson during the negotiations themselves, which were based on a single belief: free trade would prevent war. Economic relationships would promote peaceful interdependence and economic success for the United States, Britain, and the entire international community.

---

[193] McCormick, "Underlying Realities."
[194] Harry S. Truman, "Special Message to the Congress Transmitting Financial Agreement with the United Kingdom," January 30, 1946, http://www.presidency.ucsb.edu/ws/index.php?pid=12545&st=anglo&st1=agreement#axzz2fGgAglDn.
[195] James F. Byrnes, "International Trade Organization: Without Great Britain, Prospect Would Not be Bright," February 11, 1946.

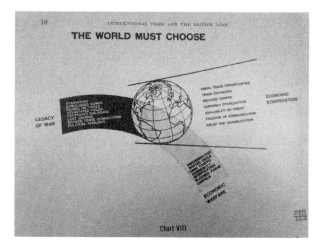

Figure 19: "The World Must Choose."
State Department officials argued that the loan would support global economic cooperation.
"International Trade and the British Loan," Washington, D.C., U.S. Department of State, 1946

Peace Bomb

Figure 20: "Peace Bomb"
Daniel Fitzpatrick in the *St. Louis Post-Dispatch* (St. Louis, MO). [196]
Americans argued that the loan to Britain was their only weapon against a world trade war.
Reprinted in "Facts on the British Loan," *The New Republic* 114, no. 10 (March 11, 1946): 332.

---

[196] Fitzpatrick was a well-known cartoonist who critiqued Conservative elites. His cartoons helped turn American public opinion against Adolf Hitler at the start of World War II and often promoted liberal issues such as equal rights for women and blacks or environmentalism. For more information, see: "Daniel Fitzpatrick," The State Historical Society of Missouri, http://shs.umsystem.edu/historicmissourians/name/f/fitzpatrick/index.html.

Truman rejoiced when the loan was endorsed by the influential Advisory Board of the Office of War Mobilization and Reconversion. His public response, issued on March 4, 1946, asserted that "the alternative to the British loan is trade warfare between nations. Peace can be built only on a foundation of world economic cooperation and stability. The British loan is a cornerstone in the world structure of peace."[197] Truman and his allies believed in international collaboration as the key to post-war harmony, informing the way they discussed the loan and advertised it to the public. Truman and Byrnes espoused multilateral cooperation among countries. Truman and his administration saw the loan as an early step in forging a post-war global political system that could ensure peace.

However, the Truman administration's endorsement did not smooth the way for the loan's approval in Congress. Truman had become increasingly unpopular by 1946. He had been ill-prepared by Roosevelt for the transition to a peacetime economy. The union movement had been strengthened during the New Deal. Returning soldiers flooded the labor pool, depressing wages. When Truman ended the wartime price controls, prices rose rapidly, wages failed to keep pace, and workers walked out in a series of strikes unprecedented in size. Oil workers struck in October, 1945. The auto, electric, meatpacking, steel, coal and rail industries were paralyzed by strikes in rapid succession by mid-1946. Truman's lack of a well-defined political agenda and his mishandling of the turbulent economic situation made him seem politically inept. The anti-Truman movement coined a popular motto that "to err is Truman," and the President's approval ratings sank. In June 1946, at the height of the loan debate in Congress, 48% of Americans said they would not vote for him as a candidate in 1948 and 46% of Americans disapproved of the way his administration was handling foreign affairs, considering heightened tensions with the

---

[197] Harry S. Truman, "Statement by the President Upon Receiving a Resolution Endorsing the British Loan Agreement," March 4, 2946, http://www.trumanlibrary.org/publicpapers/index.php?pid=1493&st=&st1=.

Soviet Union.[198] The simple fact that the Truman administration backed the loan led 58% of

Americans polled in April 1946 to oppose it.[199] Thus, Truman remained largely behind the

scenes in promoting the loan, instead allowing State Department officials Will Clayton and Dean

Acheson, along with Fred Vinson, to take the lead. He relied on these point people to do the job

of selling the loan, since it was contentious and Truman did not have the gravitas to push it

through Congress on his own.

The economic uncertainty at home also led the majority of Americans to oppose the loan,

despite the considerable concessions and requirements imposed on Britain. Americans felt they

had done their part to win the war. In their view, they supplied the weapons, money and young

men that rescued Europe. The U.S. government had spent over $50 billion in the Lend-lease

program, of which Britain had received around $31 billion. Ninety percent of these loans would

not be repaid, according to the Lend-Lease settlement negotiated alongside this new loan.

Americans were not anxious to rescue the British yet again, despite their close wartime alliance.

While the average British citizen had lived with the war for over six years, Americans considered

their own contribution to the allied effort as equally valid and substantial.

Britain also did not appear to be a trustworthy investment. It had a poor record on

international loan repayment, having defaulted in 1932 on its $4.4 billion of World War debt to

the United States.[200] In fact, Finland had been the only ally in World War I which had repaid

American loans after that war.[201] Vinson argued that "this time" would be different because "we

are making the loan on terms we believe will make repayment possible."[202] However, the

---

[198] Gallup Poll (AIPO), June 1-6, 1946, Roper Center Public Opinion Archives.
[199] Gallup Poll (AIPO), March 29-April 3, 1946, Roper Center Public Opinion Archives.
[200] Finlo Rohrer, "What's a Little Debt between Friends?" *BBC News Magazine*, May 10, 2006, http://news.bbc.co.uk/2/hi/uk_news/magazine/4757181.stm.
[201] John Lewis Gaddis, *The United States and the Origins of the Cold War, 1941-1947* (New York and London: Columbia University Press, 1972), 342.
[202] Vinson, "The British Loan," 10-11.

memory of Britain's unpaid debts combined with her presumptuous credit request offended free-market capitalist American sentiments. *The Chicago Tribune* ran articles in August 1945 upon Britain's first request for a grant entitled "The Dining Room is Closed," and "Santa Claus Dies Hard," comparing the United Kingdom to a spoiled child who took its presents for granted.[203] Would Britain ever take care of herself?

Figure 21: "Wait a minute – Why should we help this guy?"
American Nationalists argued against helping Britain, but a world trade war would threaten the U.S. just as much as it would Britain.
Herbert Block, *The Washington Post* (Washington, D.C.), 1946

[203] Clarke, *The Last Thousand Days*, 374. "The Dining Room is Closed," *The Chicago Tribune*, August 25, 1945. "Santa Claus Dies Hard", *The Chicago Tribune*, August 23, 1945.

Figure 22: "Look! He's throwing something away!"
World stability could be saved with a loan from Britain. This meant the U.S. had to avoid the isolationism of 1930, which is marked by the treacherous flag in the waterfall.
Herbert Block, *The Washington Post* (Washington, D.C.), 1946.[204]

---

[204] Herbert Block was a liberal cartoonist who defended F.D.R.'s New Deal. He worked for *The Washington Post* from 1946 to 2001, and won three Pulitzer Prizes during his career. He was most noted for his Watergate drawings, which included over 100 cartoons between June 1972 and August 1974. See: "Herblock," The Watergate Story, *The Washington Post*, http://www.washingtonpost.com/wp-

Figure 23: "But she'll never pay the fare!"
Harry Truman offers Britain a life preserver, but meets substantial Congressional opposition.
Leslie Gillbert Illingworth, *The Daily Mail* (London), March 7, 1946.
The National Library of Wales.

Even Truman's own Democratic Party was not unified in its support of the proposed

Anglo-American loan. Truman's falling polls in 1946 limited his influence among Democratic

congressmen facing a mid-term election that November. The party's majority in both houses was

threatened by Truman's unpopular policies.[205] In addition, the Southern farmers and the Northern

industrials were odd bedfellows from the beginning. [206] The growth in influence of the labor

unions during World War II further split the Democrats. Divergent interests of the Southern and

Northern Democrats prevented effective post-war economic planning.[207] By 1946, one reporter

explained that "it has become so politically popular, particularly in the House, to question

Administration motives and to vote down its requests that the temptation lingers even though the

fate of the nation and of the whole world may be at stake."[208] Keynes's belief that Vinson and

Clayton would "have to fight on…like tigers" in Congress to approve the loan was proving to be

true.[209]

Tennessee Democrat Kenneth McKellar, President pro tempore of the Senate and

Chairman of the Appropriations Committee, led Congressional supporters of the loan. Truman

did not have a Vice-President at the time, and as the senior Democrat in the Senate, McKellar

was first in the line of Presidential succession. He was invited to all wartime Cabinet meetings

for President Truman, and he acted as a right-hand man to the new President.[210] McKellar had

been a well-known Anglophobe during the inter-war period. However, he strongly supported

---

[205] In the 1946 Congressional elections, Democrats lost 54 seats in the House and 11 in the Senate, giving Republicans the majority in both houses.

[206] "Business: Cotton is King," *Time Magazine*, August 17, 1936, http://content.time.com/time/subscriber/article/0,33009,756494-2,00.html.

[207] Block, 32.

[208] Crider, "Loan to Britain tests our New World Role," *New York Times*, April 27, 1946.

[209] John Maynard Keynes, Letter to Mr. Governor Catto, October 22, 1945 King's College Cambridge, J.M.K. Papers. Thomas Silveright Catto, 1st Baron Catto was the Governor of the Bank of England from 1944 to 1949, and helped oversee its nationalization in 1946.

[210] This included cabinet meetings from April to August 1945.

Truman's agenda in the Senate in 1945, including the Anglo-American loan. His former distaste for Britain gave his support for the loan additional credibility among those on the fence.

Political views of Truman were often superseded by economic concerns in Congressmen's consideration of the loan. Many Democrats supported the agreement in order to gain access to international markets for American industry. This was a primary goal of businessman Will Clayton when he negotiated the terms of the loan. Secretary of the Treasury Fred Vinson noted that "a healthy Britain and a healthy world trade" were inextricably linked.[211] Winthrop Aldrich, President of Chase Bank and American Ambassador to the United Kingdom, argued, "The British Commonwealth should agree to do away with exchange controls on current account and give up the so called Sterling Area...relinquish the system of imperial preference and eliminate quantitative controls." [212] Aldrich was a member of the Committee on International Economic Policy, which issued a pamphlet in 1946, entitled "15 Facts on the Proposed British Loan." The pamphlet emphasized the need to "rebuild foreign trade," calling Britain "the best customer" of the United States, echoing Clayton's preoccupation with opening Britain and the Sterling Area to American exports. This argument proved convincing, and in March 1946, those few American citizens who did support the loan wanted to promote business and world trade.[213]

Figure 24: Winthrop Aldrich

[211] Vinson, "The British Loan," 13-14.
[212] Aldrich, as quoted in "Sterling-Dollar Diplomacy," *The Economic Weekly*, August 4, 1956.
[213] A majority of Americans still disapproved of the loan. Gallup Poll (AIPO), March 29-April 3, 1946, Roper Center Public Opinion Archives.

The loan's stipulation that Britain ratify the Bretton Woods agreements caused anxiety for some Democrats. Raymond Mikesell, an adviser to Assistant Treasury Secretary Harry Dexter White who helped staff the Bretton Woods Conference, argued that Britain's claims to the loan as a prerequisite of their participation in Bretton Woods meant that the United States was "paying twice for nondiscrimination" and that "Britain was blackmailing us."[214] Likewise, financiers like Winthrop Aldrich opposed Bretton Woods, which signified increased regulation of the business community, but still supported the loan for its reduction of British trade barriers. To them, the potential for increased deregulation was more tempting than the threat of increased international encroachment on finance.

Like the Democratic Party, Republicans were also plagued by internal divisions. Prior to World War II, the debate over whether to support Britain became an ideological controversy. Isolationist Senators Robert Taft of Ohio and Arthur Vandenberg of Michigan argued against involvement in the conflict, a view that was supported by groups like the America First Committee. They fought against internationalists, led by Henry Stimson, the U.S. Secretary of War. This debate continued into the 1950s, despite isolationism's apparent impracticality in the postwar era. In the Senate, Robert Taft led the Republican minority in opposition to the loan. For years, Taft had been the leader of the conservative coalition against the New Deal and labor unions. He was an avid isolationist who opposed postwar entanglements of the U.S. with other nations, such as the Bretton Woods agreements. Not only did he renounce the Anglo-American loan on principle, but he also criticized its size. He sought to undermine it at one point during the debates by introducing a much smaller, $1.25 billion alternative proposal.[215] Taft made a

---

[214] Raymond F. Mikesell, *Foreign Adventures of An Economist,* (Eugene, OR: University of Oregon, 2000), 67.

[215] Block, 73.

convincing argument, and it seemed that few Republicans would be swayed to support the financial agreement.

Figure 25: Robert Taft, "Mr. Republican"
*Time* Magazine (New York, NY), October 30, 1950.
Herbert Block, *The Washington Post* (Washington, D.C.), 1946

However, Taft was no longer joined by his fellow isolationist Senator Arthur Vandenberg. On April 22, 1946, Senator Vandenberg announced his support of the loan, marking a turning point in the negotiations. Vandenberg, formerly an ardent isolationist and opponent of the New Deal like Taft, had dramatically announced on the Senate floor his "conversion" to internationalism the prior year. Considered "the recognized spokesman of the Republican party on foreign affairs" by *The New York Times*, Vandenberg now advocated that Americans collaborate with our allies so that "our present fraternity of war becomes a new fraternity of peace."[216] He, like the Truman administration and Winston Churchill himself, saw

---

[216] McCormick, "Underlying Realities." Arthur H. Vandenberg, "American Foreign Policy," January 10, 1945, http://www.senate.gov/artandhistory/history/resources/pdf/VandenbergSpeech.pdf

Anglo-American collaboration as essential to the new world order, quoting former President Roosevelt in saying, "we must not let such differences divide us and blind us to our more important common and continuing interests in winning the war and building the peace."[217] In doing so, Vandenberg added his support of the bill to the Democratic minority in the Senate. Vandenberg became a champion of multilateralism, claiming that "this bill maybe a decisive factor in determining whether we are able to live in a world of decent commercial opportunity."[218]

One American reporter even accused Vandenberg of having "sounded like the British parliamentarians."[219] The shock of his support sent the message to many Republicans that perhaps the loan was more important than opposing Truman. Just as the loan divided British Tories, it divided U.S. Republicans between economic nationalists like Robert Taft and Leopold Amery and advocates of a multilateral approach and international collaboration like Arthur Vandenberg or Winston Churchill.

Figure 26: Arthur Vandenberg, "We either take or surrender leadership" *Time* Magazine (New York, NY), May 12, 1947

---

[217] Arthur H. Vandenberg, "American Foreign Policy," January 10, 1945, http://www.senate.gov/artandhistory/history/resources/pdf/VandenbergSpeech.pdf.

[218] Vandenberg, quoted in Anne O'Hare McCormick, "Underlying Realities."

[219] McCormick, "Underlying Realities."

Figure 27: "Aren't there certain risks involved with boating?"
Republican Senator Arthur Vandenberg promotes a lifeboat to avoid world chaos: a European Recovery Program.

<u>Figure 28:</u> Emmanuel Celler

Certain issues brought together politicians from both parties in opposition to the loan.

Zionists, who were working to create the nation of Israel, opposed the loan because of Britain's

rule of Palestine.[220] Those Jews who lived in Palestine began to resist British rule in 1939

because of Britain's suggestion that Palestine be granted independence as a primarily Arab state

with limitations on Jewish immigration.[221] European Jewish refugees who attempted to enter

Palestine were detained by the British in designated camps. Armed conflict ensued, reaching its

height in the fall of 1945. [222] Britain was forced to send over 100,000 British troops in response

to Jewish agitation in the region. This conflict promoted debate at home and abroad, American

---

[220] Rafael Medoff, "A Debt the British Paid – And One They Didn't," *The Jerusalem Post,* January 15, 2007, http://www.jpost.com/Features/A-debt-the-British-paid-and-one-they-didnt.

[221] This was proposed in the 1939 MacDonald White Paper.

[222] This conflict persisted until the United Nations Partition plan was announced on November 29, 1947, which created two separate states. The British Mandate for Palestine ended on May 14, 1948.

Jews felt personally insulted by Britain's apparent pro-Arab stance, especially in light of the recent European Holocaust. Although the loan was not directly tied to the conflict in Palestine, it was a sign of support for Britain, and helping Britain amounted to hurting the Jewish insurgents. As a result, Democrat Emmanuel Cellar, a Jewish Congressman from Brooklyn, led a crusade against the loan, arguing that financing Britain would be a de facto approval of her support for Palestine. Republican Senator Taft joined him in linking the loan debate to the negotiations on Palestine. Rabbi Stephen Wise originally led the Zionists in protesting the loan, but later voted for the loan "as an American" not a Jew, revealing how difficult it was for many Congressmen to reconcile their parochial interests with those of their nation.

Worries that the loan would support the growth of socialism in Britain also united Republicans and some Democrats in opposition. Clement Attlee's campaign promises of full employment, national health insurance, child allowances, and intense business regulation frightened American capitalists and advocates of limited government. Financier Bernard Baruch, known as "the Lone Wolf of Wall Street," warned Congress against helping other countries "nationalize their industries against us."[223] Parliament began a program of nationalizing industry in February 1946, when it bought out private shareholders of the Bank of England. In addition, the nationalization of British coal mining was well underway during the loan debate in the U.S. Congress. One congressman argued that the loan would "promote too much damned socialism at home and too much damned imperialism abroad."[224] This new government seemed untrustworthy, and as Secretary of Treasury John Snyder explained, "the Labour government was as of then untried, and it had not had an opportunity to demonstrate its capacity for national

---

[223] Kathleen Burk, *Old World, New World: Great Britain and America from the Beginning*, (London: Little Brown, 2007), 564.
[224] Emmanuel Cellar, as quoted in Clarke, *The Last Thousand Days*, 419.

leadership, much less world judgment."[225] How could this new British government be trusted to

defend capitalism and democracy?

Figure 29: "The Welfare State"
Competing political systems promoted global insecurity.
Richard Q. Yardley, *The Reporter* (New York, NY), October 11, 1949.[226]

---

[225] Jerry Hess, "The Oral History with John W. Snyder" (Harry S. Truman Library and Museum, January 15, 1969). John Snyder was Secretary of Treasury under Truman from June 1946 to 1953, following Fred Vinson.

[226] Published in Arthur Schlesinger, Jr., "The Welfare State," *The Reporter* (October 11, 1949): 28-29 http://www.unz.org/Pub/Reporter-1949oct11-00028. In this article, Schlesinger critiques Herbert Hoover and his fellow conservatives for "find[ing] favors so reprehensible when bestowed by government upon farmers or workers, and so beneficial when bestowed on business." *The Reporter* was run by Maz Ascoli, a noted anti-fascist who strongly supported the advocacy of American democracy and capitalism abroad. Schlesinger was a prominent historian who authored *The Vital Center* (1949), which advocated The New Deal as a moderate choice between unregulated capitalism and Henry Wallace's liberalism. A professor at Harvard from 1945-1961, he wrote extensively on Andrew Jackson, Franklin Roosevelt, and John Kennedy, including the three volume *The Age of Roosevelt*. He was awarded the Pulitzer Prize twice, as well as The Bancroft Prize in 1958. He was also an avid Democrat who worked as Adlai Stevenson's primary speechwriter in the 1952 and 1956 elections, later working for Robert Kennedy in 1968 and George McGovern in 1972. He was a "court historian" for John F. Kennedy, which resulted in *A Thousand Days: John F. Kennedy in the White House*. For more information see: "Arthur M. Schlesinger, Jr.", Encyclopedia Britannia, http://www.britannica.com/EBchecked/topic/527608/Arthur-

United States opposes bilateral trading because it

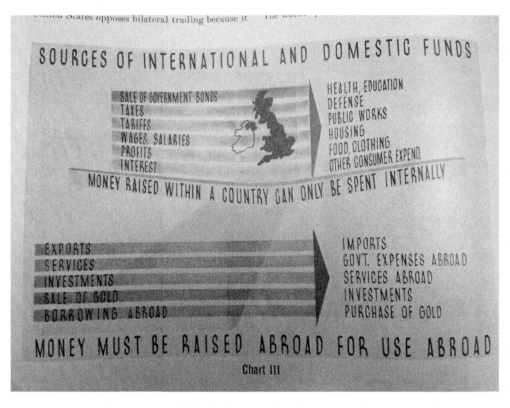

# SOURCES OF INTERNATIONAL AND DOMESTIC FUNDS

SALE OF GOVERNMENT BONDS
TAXES
TARIFFS
WAGES, SALARIES
PROFITS
INTEREST

HEALTH, EDUCATION
DEFENSE
PUBLIC WORKS
HOUSING
FOOD, CLOTHING
OTHER CONSUMER EXPEND.

MONEY RAISED WITHIN A COUNTRY CAN ONLY BE SPENT INTERNALLY

EXPORTS
SERVICES
INVESTMENTS
SALE OF GOLD
BORROWING ABROAD

IMPORTS
GOVT. EXPENSES ABROAD
SERVICES ABROAD
INVESTMENTS
PURCHASE OF GOLD

## MONEY MUST BE RAISED ABROAD FOR USE ABROAD

Chart III

Figure 30: "Sources of International and Domestic Funds."
U.S. State Department Pamphlet explains that the loan would not finance domestic socialist programs in Britain.
"International Trade and the British Loan," Washington, D.C., U.S. Department of State, 1946

Truman supporter Dean Acheson addressed this concern by explaining that American dollars would not be used to finance British domestic payments, emphatically arguing "it doesn't need to come to U.S. for its own currency."[227] This argument was also considered in a chart from a State Department pamphlet on the loan, which lists the sources and uses of international funds versus domestic funds, with the captions: "Money raised within a country can only be spent internally," and "Money must be raised abroad for use abroad."[228] This was an

M-Schlesinger-Jr.
[227] Acheson, 15-16.
[228] See appendix, Image 19. "International Trade and the British Loan," (Washington, D.C., U.S.

oversimplification, because sterling-dollar convertibility would allow Britain to use proceeds domestically and the loan would lend credibility to the Labour government and its policies.

Perhaps the biggest fear for many Americans was that other countries would line up for their own loans. *Time* reported that on Capitol Hill that there was some "squawking" that a loan to England would prompt similar requests from other countries.[229] Bernard Baruch argued that "if we let England have billions, we will have to let Russia, China, France, Norway, Denmark, Belgium…"[230] All American allies would have the opportunity to come knocking for a hand out. Vinson claimed that Britain was a special scenario because of the history of Anglo-American collaboration and because "no other nation plays the part in world trade plays," but rumors surrounding a potential Soviet loan and France's request in 1946 fueled political pressure to help more allies.[231] Eleanor Roosevelt told Truman to issue two loans: one to Britain and one to the Soviet Union, "to promote world cooperation."[232] Senator Vandenberg agreed, saying to his advisor John Foster Dulles, "It seems to me, if we grant a loan to England and deny one to Russia (if she asks for it as she undoubtedly will) we have thereby made further cooperation among 'The Big Three' practically impossible (which incidentally, would be the end of UNO)."[233] The question of how a British loan could be issued without insulting other allies, especially the Soviet Union, remained unanswered.

---

Department of State, 1946).

[229] Rafael Medoff, "A Debt the British Paid – And One They Didn't," *The Jerusalem Post*, January 15, 2007, http://www.jpost.com/Features/A-debt-the-British-paid-and-one-they-didnt.

[230] Bernard Baruch, quoted in Gardner, *Sterling Dollar Diplomacy*, 194.

[231] Vinson, "The British Loan," 14.

[232] George C. Herring, Jr., *Aid to Russia*, 253. See Eleanor Roosevelt to Truman, November 20, 1945, cited in Gardner, *Architects*, 129.

[233] John Foster Dulles would later serve as a Republican Senator in 1949 and as the 52nd U.S. Secretary of State from 1953-1959. Vandenberg, as quoted in Herring, 253.

Henry Wallace, Roosevelt's former Vice President and now Secretary of Commerce, supported the British loan precisely because it would open the door to other loans. Well-known for his leftist tendencies, he was mistrusted by many of the more conservative Southern Democrats, who disliked his progressive politics. As a result, Roosevelt had replaced him with Truman as his vice presidential candidate in 1944. Still, Wallace sided with the Truman administration and negotiator William Clayton by arguing that "without this aid in the rehabilitation of its economy, the British government would have been forced to adopt totalitarian trade methods and economic warfare of a sort which would have closed the markets of much of the world to American exports."[234] Still,

Wallace did not seem fully invested during the loan negotiations. *Time* Magazine reported, "Henry Wallace bothers the British experts. They know he is sympathetic to their case, but when he closes his eyes and seems to doze, the British get uneasy. Old Washington hands could tell them that when Wallace falls into this trance-like attitude it really indicates intense interest."[235] This palpable disinterest was due to his real desire for the passage of a Soviet loan in addition to the British loan.

Figure 31: Henry Wallace

[234] Henry A. Wallace, "The Way to Peace: Division of World Between Russia and the United States," http://newdeal.feri.org/wallace/haw28.htm. A speech delivered before a meeting under the joint auspices of the National Citizens Political Action Committee and the Independent Citizens Committee of the Arts, Sciences, and Professions, New York, N.Y., September 12, 1946. *Vital Speeches of the Day* (October 1, 1946), v. 12, n. 24, p. 738.
[235] "Economics: Salesman Wanted," October 18, 1945, *Time Magazine*, http://content.time.com/time/magazine/article/0,9171,776244,00.html.

The French would get the first loan after the British. In April 1946, France requested a

$500 million loan from the United States to fund a large dollar deficit caused by excessive

imports from America.[236] The Truman administration referred the request to the Export-Import

bank, which had access to only $1 billion to support American economic growth by insuring or

financing the purchase of American exports by foreign governments unable to take on risk.[237]

Still, William Clayton took this request seriously since he considered Britain and France to be

the "key to the whole Western European situation."[238] The French legislative elections were

scheduled for June 2, 1946, and with its unstable political and economic prospects, it seemed

likely that the French communist party would gain some ground.[239] As a result, Clayton

recommended that the loan be increased to $650 million to revitalize French support for alliance

with the Americans. The final agreement included a $650 million loan for 1946-1949 with $250

million to be drawn upon at a later date.[240] In return, France agreed to relax its import duties,

privatize trade, and end other interventionist trade policies like government purchases of French

exports.[241] For example, French cinemas would no longer limit the number of foreign films that

could be shown a year.[242] Unlike the British agreement, this loan was made through the Export-

Import Bank, eliminating the need for Congressional approval and was thus completed on May

28, 1946.[243]

---

[236] Anthony Carew, *Labour Under the Marshall Plan: The Politics of Productivity and the Marketing of Management Science* (Wayne State University Press, 1987), 31.

[237] It was established in 1934.

[238] Will Clayton, quoted in Herring, 266.

[239] The Communist PCF (*Parti communiste français*) did receive the most popular votes in the election, at 28%. A three-party coalition was elected, which constituted of the Christian Democrats, Communists, and PCF parties. However, after PCF leader Maurice Thorez insisted on leading the government, he and his other party members were dismissed. See: Herring, 266.

[240] Carew, 32.

[241] Carew, 32.

[242] This Blum-Byrnes Film Agreement was signed in the United States on the same date the loan was approved. See also: Jens Ulff-MØller, *Hollywood's Film Wars with France: Film-Trade Diplomacy and the Emergence of French Film Quota Policy* (University Rochester Press, 2001), 132.

[243] Herring, 266.

A loan request from the Soviet Union proved much more controversial. At the end of war, it seemed likely that the United States would continue to financially support its wartime ally, the Soviet Union, just as it was expected the United States would support Britain. The Soviets initially requested a $6 billion credit from America in January 1945, seven months before V-J day and a full nine months before the Keynes-Halifax mission. Soviet Foreign Minister Vyacheslav Molotov argued that supply aid was necessary because previous Lend-Lease negotiations with the United States had been unsatisfactory.[244] The Americans stonewalled, and Roosevelt made no comment on the request. After his death, State Department officials and President Truman refused to even acknowledge the proposal's existence.[245] Truman responded to critics, saying, a proposal "has never been officially given to me. They have never asked me for a $6 billion loan since I have been President."[246] Frustrated, the Soviet officials lowered their request to $700 million in August 1945 and made another official petition to the United Nations Relief and Rehabilitation Administration, an international relief organization that was still largely dominated by the United States. While Britain was insulted it received very little benefit from its wartime alliance with the United States during its loan negotiations, the Soviet Union was completely ignored. Its military collaboration did not yield any special treatment or legislation to satisfy its loan requests. The Soviets were told to petition international organizations to find aid.[247]

During the initial Russian requests for aid, Wallace and the president of the American Society for Russian Relief voiced their public support for a loan to the Soviet Union in speeches

---

[244] Herring, 239.

[245] "A Strange story emerges from Washington," *The New York Herald Tribune*, March 3, 1946. Quoted by Lloyd C. Gardner, *Architects*, 130.

[246] Transcript of press conference, December 7, 1945, *Public Papers of the Presidents: Harry S. Truman 1945*, p. 527. Quoted in Herring, 254.

[247] Dan Plesch, *America, Hitler, and the United Nations: How the Allies Fought World War II and Forged Peace* (London and New York: I.B. Tauris, 2011), 133.

around the country.[248] Granting Britain a loan and not Russia was an obvious snub, and Wallace wrote Truman personally, saying, "from the Russian point of view, also, the granting of a loan to Britain and the lack of tangible results on their request to borrow for rehabilitation purposes may be regarded as another evidence of strengthening of an anti-Soviet bloc."[249] Not only did Wallace think the Soviet Union deserved aid, but he also argued that their loan should be made on easier terms than the one to Britain. Unlike the British loan's substantial requirements, a Soviet loan should be made without requiring that they "agree in advance to a series of what are to them difficult and somewhat unrelated political and economic considerations."[250] He also argued for a peace treaty with the Soviet Union, which would help soothe fears of a breakdown of the alliance.

The primary reason Wallace feared giving a loan to the British and not the Soviet Union was his sense of the rising tensions between the Soviet Union and the United States. Truman's advisors had cautioned the new President about the dangers of underestimating the Soviet Union at the end of the war. Churchill had previously advocated a showdown with the Soviet Union while the United States still possessed an atomic advantage, but Truman failed to consider this option because of his desire to settle the tensions peacefully. In other words, Truman "was reluctant to meet the Soviet challenge head-on."[251] Soviet-American disagreement over the occupation of Japan led to the failure of the London Foreign Ministers Conference in September 1945. Afterwards, Truman admitted that he was "tired of babysitting the Soviets." [252] American exasperation with the Soviets continued to increase, and by early 1946, the threat of the

---

[248] Herring, 253.
[249] Henry Wallace, Letter to President Truman, July 23, 1946, http://historymatters.gmu.edu/d/6906/.
[250] Henry Wallace, Letter to President Truman, July 23, 1946, http://historymatters.gmu.edu/d/6906/.
[251] Gregory W. Sand, *Defending the West: The Truman-Churchill Correspondence, 1945-1960*, (Westport, CT: Praeger Publishers, 2004), 7.
[252] Leahy Diary, December 28, 29, 19145, January 1, 1946, Leahy MSS. Quoted in Herring, 260.

impending Cold War was apparent. On January 5, 1946, Truman declared that the U.S. would not recognize future communist governments. George Kennan, United States Ambassador to the Soviet Union, sent a "long telegram" in February 1946, advocating a harsher policy towards communism. Kennan explained that Soviet power was "[i]mpervious to logic of reason, it is highly sensitive to logic of force."[253] The next month, Churchill delivered his famous "Iron Curtain" speech in Fulton, Missouri, which advocated an Anglo-American alliance against the encroaching Soviet Union. Truman's hesitancy persisted, and he refused "to endorse Churchill's Fulton speech, at least not publicly," but it had become clear that U.S. policies of democratic capitalism and those of Soviet communism could not easily coexist.[254] Soviet Premier Joseph Stalin began to expand his influence abroad. He isolated Eastern Europe in the "Eastern Bloc," creating satellite governments instead of holding free and fair elections that had been promised at Yalta.[255] In addition, the Soviet Union ignored its previously announced deadline to withdraw its forces from Iran by March 2, 1946. Truman mandated that they comply, but Stalin only complied weeks later. The Soviet-Western wartime alliance was fracturing, and providing aid to Britain without addressing Russian appeals for a loan would only exacerbate the situation.

This was all too apparent to Henry Wallace. After one luncheon with Antola Gromov, the First Secretary of the Soviet Embassy in Washington, Wallace recorded that "he can't understand why we are getting ready to loan so much money to Great Britain and are not prepared to loan much to Russia…He wanted to know why Jimmie Byrnes played England's game so exclusively."[256] Wallace and his supporters sympathized with Gromov, and they too feared the

---

[253] George Kennan, "The Long Telegram," (Moscow: 22 Feb. 1946) http://www.historyguide.org/europe/kennan.html.
[254] Gregory W. Sand, *Defending the West: The Truman-Churchill Correspondence, 1945-1960*, (Westport, CT: Praeger Publishers, 2004), 7.
[255] This promise had been made during the Yalta Conference in Crimea, which was held on February 4-11, 1945.
[256] "Excerpts from the Diary of Henry A. Wallace 1945 – Into the Cold War," October 24, 1945, http://druckversion.studien-von-zeitfragen.net/Wallace%20Into%20the%20Cold%20War%201945.pdf.

growing political emphasis on the Anglo-American alliance. For example, the left-leaning *New Republic* magazine published a column in 1946 written by Earl Browder, the former head of the Communist Party of America.[257] Browder echoed Gromov's sentiments, claiming that the British loan was used as "a springboard for a campaign of hostility to the Soviet Union" and "part of an Anglo-American effort to line up the world for war against the Soviet Union."[258] Only a Soviet loan could prove that the United States was not forcing an ideological war with its international lending efforts.

Wallace also argued that Britain was not a suitable partner for the United States. He explained his sentiments, saying "to make Britain the key to our foreign policy would be, in my opinion, the height of folly. We must not let the reactionary leadership of the Republican party force us into that position. We must not let British balance-of-power manipulations determine whether and when the United State gets into war."[259] He believed that the U.S. would be best served by prioritizing Russian relations and mitigating any potential conflicts. Just as many Americans felt that Churchill had coerced them into World War II, Wallace argued that Britain's preoccupation with the Anglo-American alliance would not only dangerously antagonize the Russians but it would also leave the United States with a less than satisfactory ally.

The U.S. government did extend some direct aid for the Soviet Union's reconstruction after the war, but it continued to ignore the much larger loan requests, despite mounting protests from Russian politicians. [260] The State Department claimed Molotov's proposal had gotten lost in the files of the Foreign Economic Administrator and that it was "not really a formal request

---

[257] The editors wrote a disclaimer, saying "The *New Republic*, which believes in liberal democracy, is of course opposed on principle to communism. We publish Browder's series for its intrinsic interest and value." Earl Browder, "Report on Russia: An American Loan to the USSR," *The New Republic*, August 26, 1946, 222-225.
[258] Earl Browder, "Report on Russia: An American Loan to the USSR," *The New Republic*, August 26, 1946, 223-224.
[259] Wallace, "The Way to Peace."
[260] Herring, 239.

because the Russians did not use the standard forms and procedures required by the Export Import Bank."[261] The political side-stepping was extreme, and U.S. Ambassador to the Soviet Union Averill Harriman later acknowledged that the vagueness of the American response to the loan "added to our misunderstandings and increased Soviets' recent tendency to take unilateral action."[262] Supporters of the British loan were willing to alienate Russia in order to achieve their goals.

Thus, the start of formal negotiations on a potential $1 billion credit for the Soviet Union were delayed until March 1946, only four days before the Anglo-American Financial Agreement hearings began in the Senate Banking and Currency Committee. The Soviet Union walked out of the negotiations because of the substantial conditions for a loan proposed by the United States, including a "greater voice for the United States in assisting the peoples of Eastern Europe to 'solve by democratic means their pressing economic problems'," a treaty of friendship, and the elimination of trade barriers.[263] The economic terms were similar to those imposed on the British loan, but Russia was more committed to opposing multilateral trade and less desperate for American aid than Great Britain, in part because it had already resigned itself to a smaller loan from the United Nations. Instead, the two countries came to a compromise, and the Soviet Union abandoned its $700 million proposal to both the U.S. government and UNRRA and to allow international agencies to supervise the relief efforts, and the United States recommended that the United Nations Relief and Rehabilitation Administration distribute $250 million to the "independent" Soviet Republics of Ukraine and Byelorussia.[264]

---

[261] Herring, 225.
[262] Harriman memorandum, November 14, 1945. Quoted in Herring, 259.
[263] Secretary of State to Charge of the Soviet Union, February 21, *FR, 1946,* VI, 828-829. See also: Herring, 261-262.
[264] The Soviet Union's lend-lease debt was not settled until 1972, when Nixon visited Moscow. Herring, 244.

In the end, deteriorating Soviet-American also ended up being a strong motivator for Congress to approve the Anglo-American loan. The Soviets had requested a loan well before the British and French did. Additional foreign loan requests like this fueled the greatest initial opposition to the Anglo-American loan. However, as U.S.-Soviet relations worsened and anti-communist rhetoric in American heated up, the British promoted their loan as a way to shore up the capitalist West against the communists in Russia.

Winston Churchill himself was soon charming the Americans while spreading fear of the Soviets. After his March 15, 1946, the "Iron Curtain" speech, Churchill visited Washington and New York to help make the British case for the loan at Lord Halifax's request. Halifax hoped Churchill's celebrity would sway loan opponents in the United States. Halifax wrote to Winston on the eve of his visit, "You will get a very warm welcome from all your American friends, who are still frankly puzzled at what seemed to them the great ingratitude of the British people."[265] Churchill was far from a socialist, and he had spearheaded a historic collaboration with Roosevelt. Despite some American resentment towards his war-mongering ways, Winston seemed to be the most trust-worthy of the ungrateful Englishmen.

Halifax arranged for Churchill to meet with prominent New York financier Bernard Baruch, who believed that the loan would dangerously support British socialism. On February 8 1946, Halifax sounded desperate:

> I don't know whether you might feel like saying anything to him about the Loan. I have no doubt in my mind that it would be the best settlement we could get, and the world will drift into a sad mess if it is rejected, and many other consequences not good for Anglo-American relations would also in my judgment follow. Bernie is taken somewhat as a prophet on these matters, but he has as great veneration for you as he has for Keynes. And that's saying a lot.[266]

---

[265] Lord Halifax, Letter to Winston S. Churchill, December 3, 1945, Churchill Papers, Churchill College Archive, Cambridge.

[266] Lord Halifax, Letter to Winston Churchill, February 8, 1946, Churchill Papers, Churchill College Archive, Cambridge.

Churchill reported back in a March 19th telegram to Attlee that Baruch, originally a staunch opponent of the loan, would not "take any action against" it because "he considers that the Russian situation makes it essential that our countries stand together. He is of course in full agreement with me on that."[267] Their meeting had been so successful that apparently Baruch even "spoke last night to me in the sense that he might urge that the Loan should be interest-free as a gesture of unity."[268] This change of heart stemmed not from Churchill's celebrity, but from the changing "Russian situation." The shift in Soviet relations with the West clearly altered the way the British loan was viewed by Americans and British alike. Many Congressmen, like Baruch, came to support the loan as an attempt to ensure capitalism's dominance over communism.[269] Suddenly, the British Labour Party's welfare state and socialist policies did not seem as much of a threat. While, the Soviets were initially the main reason not to approve the British loan, they rapidly evolved into the best reason to do the opposite.

---

[267] Winston S. Churchill, Telegram, March 19, 1946, Churchill Papers, 2/4, Churchill College Archives, Cambridge.

[268] Winston S. Churchill, Telegram, March 19, 1946.

[269] Between the loan's December 1945 passage in Parliament and July 1946 passage in Congress, Churchill made his "iron curtain" speech in Fulton, George Kennan sent his "long telegram" detailing why the Soviet Union needed to be contained, and the United States had stopped delivering supplies to East Germany. See: Gardner, *Architects,* 128.

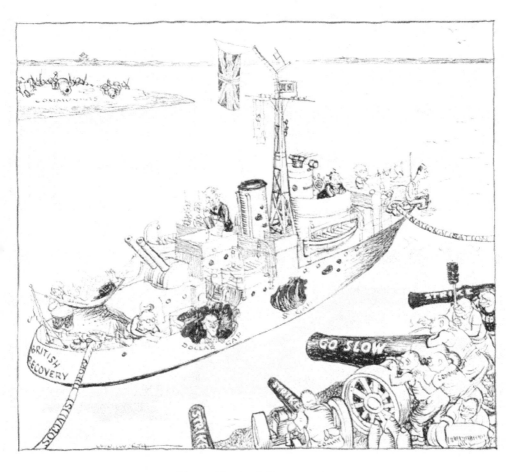

Figure 32: "Socialist Theory."
The ship of "British Recovery" is moored by "Socialist Theory" and "Nationalisation," but has two holes labeled "dollar gap." Communists look ready to strike. Without dollars to finance imports, the British economy was in grave danger. Communism could take hold as British citizens became more and more desperate.
Leslie Gillbert Illingworth, *The Daily Mail* (London), 1947.
The National Library of Wales.

The final hurdle for the loan in the Senate was a loans-for-bases amendment proposed by Democratic Senator Ernest McFarland. The proposal advocated a renegotiation with Britain for military bases in exchange for the loan, an idea that Britain was highly unlikely to accept.[270] After Vandenberg's April 22nd speech in favor of the loan, many Republicans followed his lead in striking down the amendment. It lost by only 5 votes on May 8, 1946.[271] The loan itself passed the Senate with an almost even split of 46 to 34 two days later.[272] The Committee on Banking and Currency then recommended approval in the House after an intense month of interrogation. Republican Representative Everett Dirksen prompted debate with a proposal that the British provide adequate collateral to secure the loan, but it was rejected 166 to 112.[273] Finally, the House approved the loan's funding with a vote of 219 to 155 on July 13, 1946. $3.75 billion was transferred to the British Treasury, almost a year after Keynes and Halifax had come to Washington.

The Anglo-American Loan Agreement highlighted the extreme tensions present in American domestic politics at the time. Both the Americans and British could hardly praise the passage of the loan. Britain felt exploited after making substantial economic concessions, and while the American negotiators had been more successful than Keynes and Halifax, the Congressional debates reveal many politicians' profound discontent with the Truman

---

[270] McFarland was a Senator from Arizona who later served as the state's governor and Chief Justice of the Arizona Supreme Court. He is largely responsible for the success of the 1944 G.I. Bill. McFarland argued that obtaining ownership of naval bases currently leased from the British would mitigate the risk that American enterprises would continue to be discriminated against in the British Empire. During the war, the bases had been leased to the United States for only military purposes, and full ownership would give the United States commercial rights to the bases.

[271] The final vote was 45 to 40. Over a third of Democrats and half of Republican senators voted with McFarland. See: "Senate Vote #138 in 1946," Govtrack.us, https://www.govtrack.us/congress/votes/79-1946/s138.

[272] 29 Democrats and 17 Republicans voted for the loan, while 15 Democrats and 18 Republicans voted against it. See: "Senate Key Votes – 1946," *Congressional Quarterly News Features*, 1955, http://library.cqpress.com/cqalmanac/file.php?path=CQ%20Key%20Votes%20Tables/1946_Senate_Key_Vote_Tables.pdf&PHPSESSID=riro0n7d4remtkkn9o6r9brov3.

[273] Phillip A. Grant, "President Harry S. Truman and the British Loan Act of 1946," *Presidential Studies Quarterly* 25, no. 3 (Summer 1995): 489-496, http://www.jstor.org/stable/27551463.

Administration's foreign affair policy. Just as the British debates were more complicated than they first appear, both Republicans and Democrats were divided in their stance on the loan. The Anglo-American alliance had been completely reevaluated, and the loan negotiations and debate forced both countries to redefine their international policies. Britain relinquished its protectionist economic agenda in return for the political and financial support of the United States. The United States committed to a role as international enforcer of multilateralism, embracing its role as leader of the Western Alliance in a manner that required economic, diplomatic, and military measures. The loan is an example of the United States using economic assistance as a Cold War weapon, since shoring up British support was vital in the face of Soviet expansionism. In addition, it set a precedent for promoting international trade as a means to secure peace, which would later result in the 1947 Marshall Plan.[274]

---

[274] The Marshall Plan was announced in June 1947 and enacted in 1948. It resulted in $13 billion of American assistance for Europe intended to help combat the spread of Soviet communism.

Figure 33: "Loan to Britain".
Prime Minister Clement Attlee prepares to marry a woman named "Loan to Britain." Lord Halifax and John Maynard Keynes are bridesmaids, and Truman holds a man, labeled "G.I. Congress Joe," at gunpoint to give away the bride.
Leslie Gilbert Illingworth, *The Daily Mail* (London), February 5, 1946.
The National Library of Wales.

## Chapter Five: The Afterlife of the Loan

The Anglo-American Loan of 1946 brought Britain and the U.S. into a wholesale restructuring of the post-war economic order. "The loan convinced the United States of the importance of partnership with the British in the face of the deteriorating Soviet-American alliance. The ratification of the loan...ended a cycle of unprecedented American controversy about Britain, its Socialist experiment, its role in world affairs, its claim to help from the United States...Britain is becoming, more than ever, an integral part of the inner-American political struggle," one British journalist wrote.[275] It promoted increased economic integration, as well as a guarantee of political partnership and stability in what *The Pittsburgh Press* called "a jittery world."[276] By tying Bretton Woods membership to the loan, the U.S. Congress forced Britain, then the world's second largest economy, to subscribe to its principles. Without the loan, Britain was much less likely to have joined, and the world economy would have evolved differently.[277] The United States had also proved itself as a loyal and useful ally to Britain by offering her the financial cushion necessary to meet Bretton Woods' requirements, and Britain now publicly subscribed to American principles of free trade.

Thus, the Anglo-American partnership had been fundamentally renegotiated. A year earlier, Britain assumed it wielded the same sway and international influence as its American partners. By the loan's implementation, however, it was clear that the United States held the upper hand. British Diplomat John Balfour wrote to the Foreign Office, "the dollar sign is back in the Anglo-American equation."[278] Emotional attachment did not guarantee economic or

---

[275] Gunther Stein, "America Appraises Britain," *The Spectator*, March 7, 1947. http://archive.spectator.co.uk/article/7th-march-1947/7/america-appraises-britain.

[276] "We are on the Spot," *The Pittsburgh Press*, July 12, 1946, 12. http://news.google.com/newspapers?nid=1144&dat=19460712&id=qgkeAAAAIBAJ&sjid=zkwEAAAAIBAJ&pg=1705,4755944.

[277] The Bretton Woods currency system would enhance world trade and prevail until an inflation crisis caused Nixon to take the U.S. off the gold standard in 1971.

political collaboration. Britain was not the international creditor she used to be, and she gave up her few bargaining chips (such as control of the Sterling Area) by joining the Bretton Woods agreements. Britain slowly began to recognize the shift of global economic and political power to the United States after accepting the American terms of the loan, and as Keynes explained, "Two days in Westminster are enough to teach one what a vast distance separates us here from the climate of Washington."[279]

The grueling negotiations and approval process had dismantled the niceties of international relations and revealed each side's concerns during this period of intense uncertainty. Once the loan passed Congress, Chancellor of the Exchequer Hugh Dalton wrote in his diary, "the getting of the American Loan has lifted heavy immediate anxieties. It has also already made a subtle difference to one's whole attitude towards the Americans. One feels one can now speak much more frankly to them, particularly when expressing disagreement."[280] Britain would no longer naively underestimate the force of the United States in pursuing its national interests. This partnership would not exist without substantial gains for each party. Americans' knowledge of Britain's desperate economic situation gave them the opportunity to push their international agenda, at Britain's expense. Power politics, not emotional allegiance, would rule the post-war order.

Despite warnings from the loan's critics, the real implications of its stipulations were not fully apparent to British politicians until more than a year after the funds were transferred. Because of the agreement's complicated and vague language, many Parliamentarians believed future negotiations would yield a more flexible arrangement. This assumption was far from

---

[278] The National Archives, Foreign Office 115/4225, Balfour to Foreign Office, August 21, 1945. Quoted in Wevill, 53.

[279] John Maynard Keynes to Parliament. Quoted in Peter Clarke, *The Last Thousand Days*, 343.

[280] Hugh Dalton, Diary, August 1, 1946, Hugh Dalton Archives, London School of Economics and Political Science.

unwarranted; "The application of the principles set forth in this section shall be the subject of full consultation between the two governments should as occasion may arise," the loan proposal read.[281] Although the negotiations had been harsh, the long-standing Anglo-American partnership promoted an implicit trust in the United States that still persisted for many Parliamentarians. British loan supporters held out hope for a possible friendly interpretation of the conditions, regarding the requirements as general guidelines rather than strict obligations.

This confusion stemmed in part from the loan's many functions. It not only served as an extension of credit, but was also tied to Lend-Lease, Bretton Woods, the International Trade Conference of 1946, and informed the commercial policy of both countries. The terms of these connections were unclear, so it was reasonable for British politicians to assume that the requirements could be interpreted to a more amicable degree. The two countries had agreed to "mutually advantageous" policy of trade liberalization, implying that much more breathing room existed for its implementation than was actually available.[282] Dalton confessed, "I have always thought, though I have not ventured to say so except to very few, that once the Loan was through we should have no real difficulty with the American 'conditions,' many of which could be interpreted or rediscussed with the U.S. to suit any genuine British necessities."[283] The openly principled nature of the American conditions made British skeptical of their feasibility.

For example, the loan's "waiver of interest" clause provided British politicians with an escape clause in times of economic stress, supporting the preconception that Americans would be

---

[281] "Financial Agreement," December 6, 1945, *Anglo-American Financial and Commercial Agreements*, Department of State Publication 2439, Commercial Policy Series 80, p. 9. https://fraser.stlouisfed.org/docs/historical/martin/17_07_19451206.pdf.

[282] "Statement by President Truman and Prime Minister Attlee," December 6, 1945, *Anglo-American Financial and Commercial Agreements*, Department of State Publication 2439, Commercial Policy Series 80, p. 1. https://fraser.stlouisfed.org/docs/historical/martin/17_07_19451206.pdf. See also: Thomas W. Zeiler, "GATT Fifty Years Ago: U.S. Trade Policy and Imperial Tariff Preferences" (University of Colorado at Boulder), 710, http://www.langinnovate.msu.edu/~business/bhcweb/publications/BEHprint/v026n2/p0709-p0717.pdf.

[283] Hugh Dalton, Diary, January 8, 1946, Hugh Dalton Archives, London School of Economics and Political Science.

flexible regarding the loan's implementation. The agreement also included a generous settlement for Lend-Lease aid, concluding that the United Kingdom pay for any remaining American property in Britain and for the wartime aid with $650,000,000. In effect, this allowed Britain to pay for only 10% of the materials it had received. Lastly, the United Kingdom agreed to transfer sterling to the United States at its request prior to 1951 (but not more than $50,000,000) for the U.S. to use only to purchase land or construct buildings in the British Empire. Each of these requirements reinforced the lingering argument that the United States would accommodate Britain's dire economic situation in the loan's implementation.

Additionally, the loan proposal included an optimistic joint document on "Proposals for Consideration by an International Conference on Trade and Employment," a proposed meeting to create a UN-sponsored trade organization that would limit trade barriers (i.e. restrictions, subsidies, state trading, and cartels).[284] Britain agreed to "generally to move forward with the United States and other countries toward the common objective of expanded multilateral trade" by signing the loan agreement, and that included endorsing the November 1947 United Nations Conference for further discussion of international cooperation in Havana.[285] This obligation was deemed insignificant by the British, since, as one Labour politician argued, "in the circumstances of the world today, an international trade agreement, making all world trade free, which is substantially the basis of this agreement [the loan] is impossible…I think this trade agreement will turn out to be manifestly unworkable, when they come down to confer I believe that the international trade conference will come to nothing at all."[286] This politician was right, and the proposed International Trade Organization was indeed never ratified. However, many elements

---

[284] The document was optimistic because a successful conference seemed unlikely, especially considering the substantial debates on international trade policies that had already occurred during the loan negotiations.

[285] "Statement by President Truman and Prime Minister Attlee," December 6, 1945.

[286] "Anglo-American Loan Agreement," (The House of Commons, July 19, 1946), vol425 cc1611-46, http://hansard.millbanksystems.com/commons/1946/jul/19/anglo-american-loan-agreement.

of its charter, including the 45,000 tariff concessions that were negotiated, were encompassed in the General Agreement on Tariffs and Trade, which lowered tariffs and promoted free trade in January 1948.[287] GATT remained the primary multilateral legal document governing international trade until the formation of the World Trade Organization in 1995. Britain signed itself up to support a global multilateral agenda for years to come.

The agreement also forbade the United Kingdom from receiving loans from other members of the British Commonwealth after December 6, 1945 and before 1951 "on terms more favorable to the lender than this line of credit."[288] This was a direct offense to a potential Canadian loan to Britain, which had been proposed even before that of the United States, in August 1944. The President of the Bank of Canada, Graham Towers, even visited Washington when the negotiations seemed stalled in October 1945 to discuss the loan with Keynes, but besides him, "those of us in Ottawa concerned with these international financial arrangements were not aware of the course of the Anglo-American negotiations," let alone had any "influence on them."[289] This clause meant that the Anglo-Canadian negotiations had to begin on the American loan's terms, a "surprise [that] caused serious resentment in Ottawa."[290] After the American negotiations, several British officials visited Ottawa on December 8, 1945 to discuss the conditions, and a $1.25 billion loan was signed in early March 1946.[291]

The Canadian loan would be repayable over a period of twenty years (from 10 years after the end of the war) at only 2 per cent interest, and included a "waiver of interest payments"

---

[287] The General Agreement on Tariffs and Trade was negotiated in Geneva in October 1947 and signed into law on January 1, 1948. The International Trade Organization had been proposed in 1945, providing inspiration for GATT, which worked to promote free trade by reducing tariffs, quotas, and subsidies.

[288] "Financial Agreement," December 6, 1945, p. 8.

[289] Robert Broughton Bryce, *Canada and the Cost of World War II: The International Operations of Canada's Department of Finance, 1939-1946* (McGill-Queen's Press, 2005): 289. Bryce was a Keynesian economist who worked for the Department of Finance from 1938-1968. See also Bryce, *Maturing in Hard Times: Canada's Department of Finance Through the Great Depression* (McGill Queen's Press, 1986).

[290] Bryce, 293.

[291] The negotiations lasted from February 11, 1946 to March 6, 1946.

clause similar to that of the American loan.[292] Canada was particularly sympathetic to Britain's plight because of its dependence on British markets for exports and its political ties to the Dominion. Still, Canada was just as dedicated to a free trade agenda as the United States because it was not a member of the Sterling Area. Canada's currency was tied to the U.S. dollar, not the pound sterling, so it had never been interested in joining the trade scheme to protect the value of British currency.[293] Canada did introduce exchange controls at the beginning of the war to prevent capital flight to the United States, but kept them favorable towards the Sterling Area.[294] Because of its immense reliance on the exportation of raw materials to Britain, as discussed by Lord Beaverbrook, Canada feared British protectionism even more than the American government did.[295] As a result, their only stipulation for the loan required that Britain and the Sterling Area not discriminate against Canadian imports.[296]

In order to more easily do business with the Sterling Area, Canada also supported American calls for sterling convertibility. In October 1947, the American Ambassador in Ottawa summarized the similar interests, saying, "in brief, it may be said that Canada today more than ever before appears ready to accept virtual economic union with the United States as a necessary substitute for the multilateralism of the Atlantic triangle now believed to have disappeared for an indefinite time to come, if not permanently."[297] Economic partnership with the United States was now a more viable opportunity for growth than continued allegiance to Britain. Canada managed

---

[292] If British gold and currency reserves fell below a certain level, payments would be deferred until they rose.

[293] Britain did not object to its exclusion because it prevented a potential flight of sterling to Canada.

[294] These controls lasted until 1953.

[295] John Killick, *The United States and European Reconstruction, 1945-1960*, (Edinburgh: Keele University Press, 1997), 40.

[296] Bryce, 284.

[297] Previously, Canada had a huge deficit with the United States and a surplus with Britain; it would export raw materials to Britain and import technology and manufactured goods from the United States. This accounts for Canada's preoccupation with keeping British markets open and its substantial American debt. Quoted in Killick, 40.

to carefully accommodate both sets of interests, and the loan passed relatively easily in both the British and Canadian Parliaments due to their amicable relationship and mutual dependence.

Despite successfully obtaining two substantial loans, it seemed Britain's economic situation was only worsening. Poor harvest in the fall of 1946, the severe winter of 1946-1947 and resultant fuel crisis, as well as increased obligations to Western Germany and rising imports to support Attlee's "full employment" policy escalated British drawings on the American loan. In early 1947, monthly withdrawals far exceeded Treasury goals of $100 million a month, and very little of the loan was actually used to finance imports from the dollar area. For example, in April 1947, $450 million of the loan was drawn in part to pay for ships.[298] The loan was being quickly spent in a successful attempt to uphold Attlee's welfare state, as well as a less successful attempt to maintain Britain's international power.[299]

In May and June 1947, Britain implemented import controls, but they were not enough to sooth fears of the international investors, who were well aware of Britain's economic struggles. The British government also severely restricted domestic capital investment, limiting modernization of the country's industries and infrastructure in favor of supporting the new welfare state.[300] By 1947, Canadian officials were concerned about the extent to which Britain had drawn on the loan, of which only $287 million remained.[301] Britain had drawn $1.45 billion of the American loan and $963 million of the Canadian loan by the end of June 1947 in order to narrowly avoid economic calamity.[302]

---

[298] Schenk, 62.
[299] Jordan became independent in May 1946, India and Pakistan followed in 1947, and Israel, Burma, and Sri Lanka left the Empire in 1948.
[300] Correlli Barnett, "The Wasting of Britain's Marshall Aid," BBC History, March 3, 2011, http://www.bbc.co.uk/history/british/modern/marshall_01.shtml.
[301] Bryce, 316.
[302] Bryce, 315.

Britain's weak economic situation became a ripe target for political upheaval both at home and abroad. The loan weakened ties within the Sterling Area and contributed to the break-up of the British Empire. Its requirements to remove trade preferences and implement convertibility reduced the advantages of trade within the colonial area relative to external trade. Countries no longer gained an economic advantage from British colonial status, allowing pre-existing nationalism and independence movements to flourish. As countries like India moved towards political independence, it was hoped by many British politicians that continued economic collaboration would safeguard many of the benefits of the empire despite increased colonial self-governance. Leopold Amery in particular espoused this idea that economic partnership was more essential than British political dominance over the empire. However, the end of the Sterling Area and attempts at sterling convertibility made obvious that economic collaboration with Britain would no longer provide many benefits to the colonies. India and Pakistan became independent on August 15, 1947, as the Indian National Congress grew more restless, appealing to previous promises of full independence after the war.[303] Jewish tensions led Britain to withdraw from Palestine in 1948, allowing the United Nations to partition it into Israel and Palestine. Malaysian independence movements stemming from Britain's inability to continue lending capital created an insurgency in 1948 that led to independence in 1957.[304] Thus, Labour's attempts at aligning the interests of England and the rest of the Sterling Area in "supporting sterling as an international currency" had failed.[305]

Domestically, the British public tired of Atlee and Labour and re-elected Churchill for a fourth term as Prime Minister in 1951. However, as some American politicians had predicted,

---

[303] John Darwin, "Britain, the Commonwealth, and the End of Empire," BBC History, March 3, 2013, http://www.bbc.co.uk/history/british/modern/endofempire_overview_01.shtml.
[304] Darwin, "Britain, the Commonwealth, and the End of Empire."
[305] Schenk, 80.

the loan allowed Britain to develop an extensive welfare state. Attlee's insistence on social welfare policies contributed to Britain's lack of negotiating power in the beginning of the loan debates. Without the loan, such hugely expensive and ambitious social programs would not have been feasible. Once begun, these entitlement programs were politically impossible to withdraw. They became a permanent fixture in each British political party's platform, and policies such as national health insurance and child allowances were advocated by even Conservative politicians. In fact, Labour's defeat was in part due to its success in fulfilling their campaign promises. Without a slogan or mission, the Labour party lost its momentum. Between this, the economic situation, and the mounting Soviet threat, Churchill was reestablished.

American citizens also reacted to the uncertain political atmosphere in domestic elections following the loan's implementation. The November 1946 elections were a referendum on Truman's first year in office, which was incredibly unpopular due to his handling of wartime price controls and the resultant labor strikes. Worsening tensions with Russia compounded the situation, and many Americans blamed Truman's poor leadership on the alliance's deterioration. After Democrats had controlled Congress for 14 years, the Republicans gained 54 seats in the House and 11 in the Senate from Democrats, taking control of both houses.

Figure 34: "U.S. Congressional Election"
Native Americans labeled Republicans, Vandenberg, Congress, and Senate, ambush the
unprepared Democrats, led by Truman and Secretary of State Byrnes, in the election of 1946.
Leslie Gilbert Illingworth, *The Daily Mail* (London), November 8, 1946.
The National Library of Wales.

The Republican win paved the way for deregulation of the American economy, which

caused an increase in the price of dollar goods.[306] This dollar inflation further concerned British

politicians regarding the impact of sterling convertibility as the British trade deficit with the

United States continued to grow. Parliamentarians anticipated the dangers of sudden

convertibility and in November 1946 began to enter into agreements with various European

Banks to try to soften the blow. These agreements would allow Britain to sell sterling to other

---

[306] Allister Hinds, *Britain's Sterling Colonial Policy and Decolonization, 1939-1958* (Westport, CT: Greenwood Publishing Group, 2001), 46.

countries in return for their bank's acceptance of sterling as a payment, essentially rewarding banks that utilized sterling as a currency.[307]

These measures did little to stop a run on sterling, and the loan's stipulation that the sterling be convertible into dollars consumed much of the remaining loan proceeds. As required, on July 15, 1947, Britain removed restrictions on payments and transfers for current transactions and made the pound convertible. This ended the dollar pool and allowed members of the Sterling Area to withdraw their sterling reserves from London. Countries with large sterling accounts rapidly sought to convert them into dollars. This gave them the ability to trade with the dollar area, which weakened economic ties within the Sterling Area.

As a result, British gold and dollar reserves were rapidly depleted and by August 16, 1947, only $850 million of the American loan remained.[308] Senator Robert Taft claimed on July 23rd that the loan was "nearly all spent on food, films, and tobacco."[309] After a quick exchange of letters, the U.S. agreed to allow Britain, as "a temporary and emergency measure," to suspend convertibility of the pound to dollar only four days later.[310] From that time on, the British were allowed to ignore this requirement of the loan. However, the economic damage had been done. On October 1, 1947, Parliament repealed the strict currency controls adopted after the Great Depression and replaced them with looser controls of the 1947 Exchange Control Act.[311] In December 1947, the U.S. Government released the remaining $400 million of the loan to Britain.[312]

---

[307] Schenk, 63. These countries included Belgium, the Netherlands, and Portugal.

[308] Bryce, 316. Convertibility was not fully implemented until December 1958.

[309] See appendix, image 6. Edmonds, 105.

[310] Bryce, 316. Convertibility was not fully implemented until December 1958.

[311] The 1939 Emergency Powers (Defence Act) included the stricter controls during the lead up to World War II. "The U.K. Exchange control: A Short History," Bank of England, http://www.bankofengland.co.uk/archive/Documents/historicpubs/qb/1967/qb67q3245260.pdf. F.A. Mann, "The Exchange Control Act, 1947," *The Modern Law Review* 10:4 (October 1947): 411-419. http://onlinelibrary.wiley.com/store/10.1111/j.1468-2230.1947.tb00062.x/asset/j.1468-2230.1947.tb00062.x.pdf;jsessionid=B29E0BDF21C3BEC87F9308CAE71AF2B8.f02t04?v=1&t=hqv3ny8a&s=879fe4fe0b4012a6e54817555e5ad3e5f2797487.

[312] Edmonds, 106.

Two years later, sterling was finally devalued, allowing for a "global realignment against the dollar."[313] Britain realized that a sudden complete return to convertibility would not be feasible. Free exchange between the sterling and dollar was very gradually restored over the next decade on a regional basis, and complete convertibility of the pound to dollars for all persons was not achieved until 1959. British exchange controls were not completely abolished by Britain in 1979.

The requirement for rapid convertibility of the sterling was a mistake because it consumed much of the dollar loan without relieving Britain's economic distress. Countries and lenders with sterling balances chose to convert to dollars rather than risk further devaluation of the sterling. It was a vote of "no confidence" in the economic prospects of Britain and its ability to repay sterling debts. However, the crisis also convinced the United States of the severity of the European dollar shortage and helped build American support for the Marshall Plan, which was under development at the time. In fact, William Clayton himself wrote a memorandum advocating European financial assistance as a necessity for American security.[314] Economic aid to foreign countries had decidedly become a political weapon for the United States.

---

[313] Schenk, 80.
[314] He submitted the memorandum in May 1946. Cochran, 193.

Figure 35: "Can we afford to help Europe?"
The bigger question for the United States is "Can we afford not to help Europe?"
Daniel Fitzpatrick, *St. Louis Post-Dispatch* (St. Louis, MO), July 20, 1947.

To the United States, the Anglo-American Loan of 1946 made obvious the economic

desperation of Britain and Europe, the U.S. advantage in economic power, and its inescapable

obligation to finance post-war reconstruction in Europe. The information exchanged during loan

negotiations gave American politicians and the public new insight into Britain's terrible

economic situation. British politicians' acceptance of such onerous conditions was evidence that

they had no alternative source of substantial funds. Additionally, the fact that the loan was

largely exhausted in one year surprised Americans, revealed Britain's economic impotency, and

implied that financial aid of much greater magnitude would be required. The United States had

unscrupulously taken advantage of the situation and forced Britain's application of American

capitalist and multilateral values on its Empire.

The loan to Britain also set a precedent for providing financial assistance to foreign

nations, in part to secure American, rather than Soviet, influence in the recipient country. In

March 1947, Truman announced that the U.S. would defend vulnerable nations against

communism, a plan that would begin with providing financial support for Greece and Turkey.

The President's personal investment in the Truman doctrine reveals how public opinion had

become more accepting of the use of financial assistance as a tool to promote American interests

abroad, especially when compared with his refusal to announce Churchill's "Iron Curtain"

speech. The 1946 loan had faced substantial criticism for its espousal of multilateral principles

and accommodation for Britain rather than the Soviet Union. Now, instead of relying on the

State Department to defend his policies, Truman felt comfortable enough to dismiss euphemisms

and figuratively declare war on the spread of communism. Also, in these new aid programs, the

United States allowed economies to gradually join the Bretton Woods structure of currency convertibility, which minimized economic dislocations. The United States had learned from its mistake with the 1946 loan.

On June 5, 1947, U.S. Secretary of State George Marshall extended Truman's ideas, and asked the U.S. to fund the reconstruction of war-torn Europe, which would result in aid to help European countries purchase food, fuel, and other imports from the United States. Two weeks later, the British and French foreign ministers invited twenty-two European nations, including the Soviet Union and its affiliated countries, to attend the Committee of European Economic Cooperation (CEEC) conference in Paris, where they could discuss a cooperative recovery plan.[315] The Soviet Union and its satellites declined to attend the CEEC conference, which later produced a "European Recover Plan," the basis for the American Marshall Plan. The CEEC found that "while aggregate overseas imports into Europe were only seven per cent above prewar in 1947, the volume of imports from the United States was 130 per cent higher than in 1938."[316] Like Britain, many European nations had very few gold and dollar reserves, limiting their ability to finance their imports. Markets across Europe struggled to finance their American deficits, and the Marshall Plan was a way to aid them in doing so.[317]

---

[315] "For European Recovery: The Fiftieth Anniversary of the Marshall Plan," http://www.loc.gov/exhibits/marshall/mars.html

[316] United Nations, Economic Commission for Europe, *A Survey of the Economic Situation and Prospects of Europe* (Geneva, 1948), xiii. Quoted in C. C. S. Newton, "The Sterling Crisis of 1947 and the British Response to the Marshall Plan," *The Economic History Review* 37, no. 3 (August 1984): 394, http://www.jstor.org.ezproxy.lib.davidson.edu/stable/2597288?seq=3.

[317] This increase in U.S. imports was mostly in "the form of relief and reconstruction goods," according to C. C. S. Newton, "The Sterling Crisis," 394.

Figure 36: "Bevin and Bidault seem to be unsure if they wish to be saved by the U.S.S. Bounty"
U.S. President Harry Truman and Secretary of State George Marshall offer French President
Georges Bidault and U.K. Secretary of State Ernest Bevin a trip on the "U.S.$. Bounty." The
recipients debate in a boat named "Paris Conference."
Leslie Gilbert Illignworth, *The Daily Mail* (London), August 21, 1947.
The National Library of Wales

Because the World Bank's lending power was capped at $2.3 billion and the International Monetary Fund was not intended for reconstruction purposes, the United States had to approve another special assistance package to prevent a European collapse, which would result in the Marshall Plan. American politicians feared that if they did not do so, chaos would ensue. The concerns that prompted the Marshall Plan's passage were markedly similar to those that supported the 1946 British loan. Even if the Soviet Union did not plan to expand its influence in the event of an economic financial meltdown, the United States' own strength was inherently tied to its ability to export to European markets.[318] If a solution was not found, multilateralism would be defeated and European countries would resort to protectionist measures like state trading and exchange controls to avoid use of the dollar.[319] Additional aid to Europe would provide more markets for American exports and help align European interests with those of the United States, just as the 1946 British loan had done.[320] The goal was to eliminate the European dollar deficit by 1951 by promoting European industry and introducing a hard line of U.S. currency. This familiar argument met much less opposition than the 1946 loan had. The British loan's precedent, combined with mounting Soviet-American tensions, paved the way for the Marshall Plan. As a result, on April 2, 1948, Congress passed the Economic Cooperation Act that funds the Marshall Plan, in large part due to its portrayal as a Cold War weapon.

Thus, the loan had also forced the Americans to decide whether the Soviet Union was a friend or foe. These reluctant allies in wartime were quickly becoming rivals in peacetime. The

---

[318] Will Clayton argued that the U.S. needed $14 billion worth of an export market a year to keep up with its level of wartime production. See: Syed Javed Maswood, *Japan and Protection: The Growth of Protectionist Sentiment and the Japanese Response* (Routledge, 2002): 32.

[319] Newton, "The Sterling Crisis," 394.

[320] Campbell Craig and Frederick Logevall, *America's Cold War: The Politics of Insecurity,* (Harvard University Press, 2009), 90.

race to Berlin had divided Europe between occupying armies. While the Soviet Union suffered terrible economic damage during the war, American politicians were reluctant to lend postwar financial aid. With the introduction of a potential Soviet loan alongside that for the British, Americans had to directly compare the merits of Britain and Soviet Union as allies. British politicians, notably Churchill in his "Iron Curtain" speech, drew sharp contrast between Britain and Soviet political systems, and anti-communist fervor was used as an excuse to fund a British loan without financing a similar loan to Russia. This was, perhaps, the beginning of the Cold War. The Marshall Plan was in effect an American economic occupation of Europe, and the Soviet Union responded with a military occupation of its allies.

Britain received by far the most aid from the Marshall Plan, amounting to about $3 billion between 1948 and 1951.[321] However, the 1946 loan proceeds and the Marshall Plan aid went mainly to sterling conversion and to social welfare, neglecting British infrastructure. Britain considered U.S. aid as a dollar deposit to use for "every conceivable thing."[322] Relatively little was spent on modernizing roads, schools, factories, and telecommunications. This failure helped the British Conservatives consolidation of power after 1951, since they promised to more efficient managers of Labour's welfare state. Still, the loan allowed for the success of Labour's campaign promises and is responsible for the lasting effects of its socialist policies, despite Britain's continued economic hardship.

The Anglo-American Loan of 1946 was a pivot point in history. The loan enabled Britain to avoid financial calamity. England's industrial plants had been either destroyed or converted to wartime production. It was deeply indebted to its colonies and the United States. Without the

---

[321] The Marshall Plan increased the amount of total aid in the form of loans or gifts from the United States to Britain in the ten years following the war to approximately $8 billion. During the military build-up related to the Korean War, Britain received an additional $986 million in aid, about half of which was non-military.

[322] Cabinet Office Memorandum, 1948, quoted in Correlli Barnett, "The Wasting of Britain's Marshall Aid."

loan, it would be economically isolated and unable to finance the imports desperately needed to feed and clothe its population. Debt default, collapse of the sterling, and domestic hyperinflation were largely avoided. The extensive stipulations imposed on Britain by the U.S. in exchange for the loan showed both the economic desperation of the former and the financial ascendancy of the latter. The world now recognized that the American era had unquestionably begun. The loan is a lens through which the rapid changes after World War II can be examined, with findings that inform international relations today and, perhaps, offer a cautionary tale to the modern United States. Immense foreign debt risks foreign demands on domestic political and economic policies.

The political and economic order of the post-war world was profoundly changed by the negotiations leading to and affects afterward of the Anglo-American Loan of 1946, which was only fully repaid by Britain on December 29, 2006.[323] After the war, the United States had found the opportunity to assert its strength, and as Republican Arthur Vandenberg explained during the loan debates, "if we do not lead, some other great and powerful nation will capitalize on our failure and we shall pay the price of our default."[324] By pushing its free trade interests in the loan negotiations, the United States set the international agenda for years to come. The "special relationship" between the United States and Great Britain, symbolized by this 1946 loan, had become defined by American hegemony.

---

[323] The waiver of payments clause was utilized in 1956, 1957, 1964, 1965, 1968 and 1976.
[324] Arthur Vandenberg, quoted in Bryce, 309.

# Bibliography

Primary Sources

"A Strange Story Emerges from Washington." *The New York Herald Tribune*, March 3, 1946.

Acheson, Dean and Fred Vinson. "The British Loan—What it Means to Us." Washington, D.C., The U.S. Department of State, January 1946.

Amery, Leopold. *The Fundamental Fallacies of Free Trade*. London: National Review Office, 1908. https://archive.org/stream/fundamentalfalla00ameruoft#page/n5/mode/2up.

Amery, Leopold. *The Washington Loan Agreements: A Critical Study of American Economic Foreign Policy*. London: Macdonald & Co. Publishers, 1946.

"Anglo-American Financial and Commercial Agreements." Washington, D.C. The U.S. Department of State. December 1945. http://fraser.stlouisfed.org/docs/historical/martin/17_07_19451206.pdf.

"Anglo-American Loan Agreement." House of Commons Debates. July 19, 1946.vol. 425 cc1611-46. http://hansard.millbanksystems.com/commons/1946/jul/19/anglo-american-loan-agreement.

"Anglo-American Financial Agreement Hearings." U.S. Congress Committee on Banking and Currency.79th Congress, 2nd Session, 1946.

"Anglo-American Financial Arrangements." House of Lords Debates. December 18, 1945. vol. 138 c777-897. http://hansard.millbanksystems.com/lords/1945/dec/18/anglo-american-financial-arrangements#S5LV0138P0_19451218_HOL_102.

Attlee, Clement. Recorded by Francis Williams. *Twilight of Empire*. New York: A.S. Barnes & Co.,1962.

Balfour, William to Foreign Office. The National Archives, Foreign Office 115/4225, August 21, 1945.

Bevan, Aneurin. "Beveridge Manifesto," *Tribune*, December 4, 1942.

Bevin, Ernest. House of Commons Debates, August 20, 1945, p. 288, John Maynard Keynes Papers, King's College Cambridge.

"Business: Cotton is King." *Time Magazine*, August 17, 1936. http://content.time.com/time/subscriber/article/0,33009,756494-2,00.html.

Byrnes, James. *All in One Lifetime*. New York: Harpers & Brothers, 1958.

Byrnes, James F. "International Trade Organization: Without Great Britain, Prospect Would Not be Bright." Speech, February 11, 1946. *Vital Speeches of the Day* 12, no. 10 (March 1946): 317.

Churchill, Winston S. *For Free Trade*. London: Churchilliana Co, 1906, 1977 reprint. http://www.churchillbooks.com/GuidePDFs/g8.pdf.

Churchill, Winston S. "The Sinews of Peace." Speech, Fulton, Missouri, Westminster College, March 5, 1946. http://www.winstonchurchill.org/learn/speeches/speeches-of-winston-churchill/120-the-sinews-of-peace.

Churchill, Winston S. "Speech at the Free Trade Hall." Manchester, England, 1904.

Churchill, Winston S. Telegram, March 19, 1946, Churchill Papers, 2/4, Churchill College Archives, Cambridge.

Churchill, Winston S. Telegram to President Truman. May 12, 1945. http://www.chu.cam.ac.uk/archives/gallery/Russia/CHAR_20_218_110.php.

Churchill, Winston S. "We Shall Fight in the Beaches." Speech, London, The House of Commons, June 4, 1940. http://www.churchill-society-london.org.uk/Dunkirk.html.

Clifford, Clark. "American Relations With The Soviet Union." September 24, 1946. Harry S. Truman Library and Museum. http://www.trumanlibrary.org/whistlestop/study_collections/coldwar/documents/sectione d.php?documentid=4-1&pagenumber=1&groupid=1.

Crider, John H. "Loan to Britain Tests Our New World Role." *The New York Times,* April 27, 1946.

Dalton, Hugh. "Anglo-American Loan (U.S. Films)." House of Commons Debates, October 15, 1946, vol. 427 c151W. http://hansard.millbanksystems.com/written_answers/1946/oct/15/anglo-american-loan-us-films#S5CV0427P0_19461015_CWA_21.

Dalton, Hugh. Diary, January 8, 1946. Hugh Dalton Archives, London School of Economics and Political Science.

Dalton, Hugh. "Washington Financial Talks." The National Archives CAB 129/5/12. November 28, 1945.

"The Dining Room is Closed," *The Chicago Tribune*, August 25, 1945.

Eisenhower, Dwight D. "Guildhall Address." Speech, London, June 12, 1945.

http://www.eisenhower.archives.gov/education/bsa/citizenship_merit_badge/speeches_national_historical_importance/guildhall_address.pdf.

Feis, Herbert. "The Conflict over Trade Ideologies." *Foreign Affairs Quarterly* 25 (January 1947). http://www.foreignaffairs.com/articles/70559/herbert-feis/the-conflict-over-trade-ideologies.

Feis, Herbert. "The Future of British Imperial Preferences." *Foreign Affairs Quarterly* 24 (July 1946). http://www.foreignaffairs.com/articles/70525/herbert-feis/the-future-of-british-imperial-preferences.

Feis, Herbert. "Keynes in Retrospect." *Foreign Affairs Quarterly* 29 (July 1951). http://www.foreignaffairs.com/articles/70903/herbert-feis/keynes-in-retrospect.

"Financial Agreement." *Anglo-American Financial and Commercial Agreements*. Department of State Publication 2439, Commercial Policy Series 80, p. 9. December 6, 1945. https://fraser.stlouisfed.org/docs/historical/martin/17_07_19451206.pdf.

Franklin, E.C. "Sterling System v. Bretton Woods and U.S. Loan." *Auckland Star*, February 7, 1946.

Gaitskell, Hugh. "More about the Loan." *The Spectator,* January 18, 1946, p. 8. http://archive.spectator.co.uk/article/18th-january-1946/8/more-about-the-loan.

Gallup Poll (AIPO), September 8-13, 1945. Roper Center Public Opinion Archives.

Gallup Poll (AIPO), March 29-April 3, 1946. Roper Center Public Opinion Archives.

Gallup Poll (AIPO), June 1-6, 1946. Roper Center Public Opinion Archives.

Harrod, Roy F. "Review of *The Washington Loan Agreements: A Critical Study of American Foreign Policy* by L.S. Amery," *International Affairs* 23:1 (January 1947).

"Harry S. Truman: His Life and Times." Harry S. Truman Library and Museum, http://www.trumanlibrary.org/lifetimes/.

Hess, Jerry. "The Oral History with John W. Snyder." Harry S. Truman Library and Museum, January 15, 1969.

"International Trade and the British Loan." Washington, D.C., U.S. Department of State, 1946.

Irving, David. "Churchill and U.S. Entry into World War II." *The Journal of Historical Review* 9, no. 3 (Fall 1989): 261-286. http://www.ihr.org/jhr/v09/v09p261_Irving.html.

Kennan, George. "The Long Telegram." Moscow, Russia. February 22, 1946. http://www.historyguide.org/europe/kennan.html.

Keynes, John Maynard. "Anglo-American Financial Agreements." December 18, 1945. Vol. 138, No. 41, King's College Cambridge, J.M.K. Papers.

Keynes, John Maynard. *The Collected Writings of John Maynard Keynes XXIV: Activities 1944-1946: The Transition to Peace*. Edited by Donald Moggridge. Cambridge, U.K.: Cambridge University Press, 1979, 2003.

Keynes, John Maynard. *The Collected Writings of John Maynard Keynes, XXVII.* Edited by Donald Moggridge. Cambridge, U.K.: Cambridge University Press, 1971-1989.

Keynes, John Maynard and Lord Halifax. "Financial Agreement Between His Majesty's Government in the United Kingdom and the Government of the United States." December 6, 1945. London: His Majesty's Stationary Office.

Keynes, John Maynard. Letter to Halifax from Keynes. August 17, 1945. King's College Cambridge, J.M.K. Papers.

Keynes, John Maynard. Letter to Mr. Governor Catto. October 22, 1945. King's College Cambridge, J.M.K. Papers.

Keynes, John Maynard. "Our Overseas Financial Prospects." August 14, 1945. King's College Cambridge, J.M. K. Papers.

"Let U.S. Face the Future: A Declaration of Labour Policy for the Consideration of the Nation." National Executive Committee of the Labour Party. April 1945.

"Loan to Britain tests our New World Role," *New York Times*, April 27, 1946.

"Lords' Loan Opposition More Vocal Than Voting." *Australian Associated Press*, December 19, 1945, p. 2. http://trove.nla.gov.au/ndp/del/article/26141061.

Lord Halifax, Edward Frederick Lindley Wood. "An English Gentleman Speaks to Americans." Speech, West Lafayette, IN, Purdue University, June 21, 1943. Indiana State Library.

Lord Halifax, Edward Frederick Lindley Wood. Letter to Winston S. Churchill, December 3, 1945. Churchill Papers, Churchill College Archive, Cambridge.

Lord Halifax, Edward Frederick Lindley Wood. Letter to Winston Churchill, February 8, 1946. Churchill Papers, Churchill College Archive, Cambridge.

Mann, F. A. "The Exchange Control Act, 1947." *The Modern Law Review* 10, no. 4 (October 1947): 411-419.

McCormick, Anne O'Hare. "British Loan as Precedent for Others," *The New York Times*,

February 13, 1946.

McCormick, Anne O'Hare. "'Underlying Realities' in the Debate on the British Loan." *The New York Times,* April 24, 1946.

Mikesell, Raymond F. *Foreign Adventures of An Economist.* Eugene, OR: University of Oregon, 2000.

*President's Economic Report for 1946.* Mimeographed copy in Harry S. Truman Papers, Files of Clark M. Clifford, Box 4. Dated January 8, 1947.

Roosevelt, Franklin D. "On Lend Lease." Speech, Washington, D.C., December 14, 1940. http://docs.fdrlibrary.marist.edu/odllpc2.html.

Sand, Gregory W. *Defending the West: The Truman-Churchill Correspondence, 1945-1960.* Westport, CT: Praeger Publishers, 2004.

"Santa Claus Dies Hard", *The Chicago Tribune*, August 23, 1945.

"Senate Vote #138 in 1946." Govtrack.us. https://www.govtrack.us/congress/votes/79-1946/s138.

"Senate Key Votes – 1946." *Congressional Quarterly News Features.* 1955. http://library.cqpress.com/cqalmanac/file.php?path=CQ%20Key%20Votes%20Tables/1946_Senate_Key_Vote_Tables.pdf&PHPSESSID=riro0n7d4remtkkn9o6r9brov3.

Stein, Gunther. "America Appraises Britain." *The Spectator*, March 7, 1947, p. 7. http://archive.spectator.co.uk/article/7th-march-1947/7/america-appraises-britain.

"Sterling-Dollar Diplomacy." *The Economic Weekly*, August 4, 1956.

Stokes, Richard. "Anglo-American Financial and Economic Discussions." House of Commons Debates, December 13, 1945, vol. 417 cc641-739. http://hansard.millbanksystems.com/commons/1945/dec/13/anglo-american-financial-and-economic.

Transcript of Press Conference. December 7, 1945. *Public Papers of the Presidents: Harry S. Truman 1945.* http://www.trumanlibrary.org/publicpapers/index.php.

Truman, Harry S. "Special Message to the Congress Transmitting Financial Agreement with the United Kingdom." Speech, Washington, D.C., January 30, 1946. http://www.presidency.ucsb.edu/ws/index.php?pid=12545&st=anglo&st1=agreement#axzz2fGgAglDn.

Truman, Harry S. "Truman Doctrine." Speech, Washington, D.C., March 12, 1947. http://avalon.law.yale.edu/20th_century/trudoc.asp.

United Nations. *A Survey of the Economic Situation and Prospects of Europe.* Economic
Commission for Europe. Geneva, 1948, xiii.

United States Department of State. *Foreign Relations of the United States: Diplomatic Papers,
1944.* Washington, D.C.: Government Printing Office, 1944.

Vandenberg, Arthur H. "American Foreign Policy." Speech, Washington, D.C., January 10,
1945. http://www.senate.gov/artandhistory/history/resources/pdf/VandenbergSpeech.pdf.

"Vinson Campaigns for British Loan." *The New York Times*, January 9, 1946.

"We are on the Spot." *The Pittsburgh Press*, July 12, 1946, 12.

Wolff, Henry-Drummond. *British Declaration of Independence.* London and New York:
Hutchinson, 1948.

Secondary Sources

Addison, Paul. *Now the War is Over: A Social History of Britain 1945-1951.* London: Jonathan
Cape Ltd, 1985.

Allen, H.C. *Great Britain and the United States: A History of Anglo-American Relations (1783-
1952).* New York: St. Martin's Press Inc., 1955.

Amenta, Edwin and Theda Skocpol, "Redefining the New Deal: World War II and the
Development of Social Provision in the United States." *The Politics of Social Policy in
the United States.* Princeton, New Jersey: Princeton University Press, 1988.

Barnett, Correlli. "The Wasting of Britain's Marshall Aid." *BBC History.* March 3, 2011.
http://www.bbc.co.uk/history/british/modern/marshall_01.shtml.

Block, Fred L. *The Origins of International Economic Disorder: A Study of United States
International Monetary Policy From World War II to the Present.* Berkeley, Los
Angeles, and London: University of California Press, 1977.

"Britain to make its final payment on World War II loan from U.S." *International Herald
Tribune,* Reprinted by *The New York Times*, December 28, 2006.

Bryce, Robert Broughton. *Canada and the Cost of World War II: The International Operations
of Canada's Department of Finance, 1939-1946.* Montreal, Quebec and Kingstown,
Ontario: McGill-Queen's Press, 2005.

Bryce, Robert Broughton. *Maturing in Hard Times: Canada's Department of Finance Through
the Great Depression.* Montreal, Quebec and Kingstown, Ontario: McGill Queen's Press,

1986.

Burk, Kathleen. *Old World, New World: Great Britain and America from the Beginning.*
     London: Little Brown, 2007.

Cardwell, Curt. *NSC 68 and the Political Economy of the Early Cold War.* Cambridge, U.K.:
     Cambridge University Press, 2011.

Carew, Anthony. *Labour Under the Marshall Plan: The Politics of Productivity and the
     Marketing of Management Science.* Detroit, MI: Wayne State University Press, 1987.

Chase, John L. "The Development of the Morgenthau Plan Through the Quebec Conference,"
     *The Journal of Politics* 16, no. 2 (May 1954): 324–59.

Clarke, Peter. *The Last Thousand Days of the British Empire: Churchill, Roosevelt, and
     the Birth of the Pax Americana.* New York: Bloomsbury Press, 2008.

Cochran, Bert. *Harry Truman and the Crisis Presidency.* New York: Funk & Wagnalls,
     1973.

Cole, G.D.H. *The Post-War Condition of Britain.* London: Routledge and Kegan Paul,
     1956.

Collins, Edward H. "Economics and Finance: 'The Dollar Gap' – Gone or Just Obscured?" *The
     New York Times,* November 27, 1950.

Craig, Campbell and Frederick Logevall. *America's Cold War: The Politics of Insecurity.*
     Cambridge, MA: Harvard University Press, 2009.

Darwin, John. "Britain, the Commonwealth, and the End of Empire." *BBC History.* March 3,
     2011. http://www.bbc.co.uk/history/british/modern/endofempire_overview_01.shtml.

Edmonds, Robin. *Setting the Mould: The United States and Britain 1945-1950.* New
     York and London: W.W. Norton and Company, 1986.

"First World War." National Archives Exhibitions.
     http://www.nationalarchives.gov.uk/pathways/firstworldwar/aftermath/brit_after_war.ht
     m.

Foot, Michael. *Aneurin Bevan: A Biography, Volume 2: 1945-1960.* London: Faber and Faber,
     2009.

"For European Recovery: The Fiftieth Anniversary of the Marshall Plan," The Library of
     Congress, http://www.loc.gov/exhibits/marshall.

Forrestal, Gregory. *Our Finest Hour: Will Clayton, the Marshall Plan, and the Triumph of*

*Democracy*. Stanford, C.A.: Hoover Institution Press, 1993.

Freeland, Richard M. *The Truman Doctrine and the Origins of McCarthyism: Foreign Policy, Domestic Politics, and Internal Security: 1946-1948*. New York: Alfred A. Knopf, 1972.

Gaddis, John Lewis. *The United States and the Origins of the Cold War, 1941-1947*. New York and London: Columbia University Press, 1972.

Gannon, Philip. "The Special Relationship and the 1945 Anglo-American Loan." *Journal of Transatlantic Studies* 12, no. 1 (April 2014): 1-17.

Gardner, Lloyd C. *Architects of Illusion.* Chicago: Quadrangle Books, 1970.

Gardner, Richard N. *Sterling Dollar Diplomacy: The Origins and the Prospects of Our International Economic Order*. New York: McGraw-Hill Book Company, 1969.

Grant, Philip A. "President Harry S. Truman and the British Loan Act of 1946." *Presidential Studies Quarterly* 25, no. 3 (Summer 1995): 489-496. http://www.jstor.org/stable/27551463.

Harris, Kenneth. *Attlee*. New York and London: W.W. Norton & Company, 1982.

Harrod, Roy. *The Life of John Maynard Keynes*. New York: Harcourt, Brace & Howe, 1951.

Herring, Jr., George C. *Aid to Russia 1941-1946: Strategy, Diplomacy, and the Origins of the Cold War*. New York: Columbia University Press, 1973.

Hathaway, Robert. *Ambiguous Partnership: Britain and America, 1944-1947*. New York: Columbia University Press, 1981.

Hinds, Allister. *Britain's Sterling Colonial Policy and Decolonization, 1939-1958*. Westport, CT: Greenwood Publishing Group, 2001.

Martincová, Ing. Marta. "Roy Forbes Harrod." *BIATEC* 10 (December 2002): 25-28. http://www.nbs.sk/_img/Documents/BIATEC/BIA12_02/25_28.pdf.

Killick, John. *The United States and European Reconstruction, 1945-1960*. Edinburgh, U.K.: Keele University Press, 1997.

Kindleberger, Charles R. *A Financial History of Western Europe*. London: George Allen & Unwin, 1984.

MacKercher, Brian J. C. *Transition of Power*. Cambridge, U.K.: Cambridge University Press, 1990.

Maswood, Syed Javed. *Japan and Protection: The Growth of Protectionist Sentiment and the*

*Japanese Response.* New York: Routledge, 2002.

Medoff, Rafael. "A Debt the British Paid – And One They Didn't." *The Jerusalem Post,* January 15, 2007. http://www.jpost.com/Features/A-debt-the-British-paid-and-one-they-didnt.

Meyer, Sir Christopher. *Mortgaged to the Yanks.* Takeaway Media, 2007.

Morgan, Kenneth O. *Britain Since 1945: The People's Peace.* Oxford University Press, 2001.

Newton, C. C. S. "The Sterling Crisis of 1947 and the British Response to the Marshall Plan." *The Economic History Review* 37, no. 3 (August 1984): 391-408. http://www.jstor.org/stable/2597288.

Ovendale, Ritchie. *The English-Speaking Alliance: Britain, the United States, the Dominions and the Cold War 1945-1951.* London: George Allen & Unwin Ltd., 1985.

Parmar, Inderjeet. *Special Interests, the State and the Anglo-American Alliance, 1939-1945.* London and Portland, OR: Frank Cass, 1995.

Paterson, Thomas G. "The Abortive Loan to Russia and the Origins of the Cold War, 1943-1946." *The Journal of American History* 56, no. 1 (June 1969): 70-92.

Plesch, Dan. *America, Hitler, and the United Nations: How the Allies Fought World War II and Forged Peace.* London and New York: I.B. Tauris, 2011.

Roberts, Andrew. "A History of the English-Speaking Peoples since 1900." London: Weidenfeld & Nicolson, 2006; New York: HarperCollins Publishers, 2007.

Rodgers, Daniel T. *Atlantic Crossings: Social Politics in a Progressive Age.* Cambridge and London: The Belknap Press of Harvard University Press, 1998.

Rosenson, Alex. "The Terms of the Anglo-American Financial Agreement." *The American Economic Review* 37, no. 1 (March 1947): 178–187. http://www.jstor.org/stable/1802868.

Rosenof, Theodore. "The American Democratic Left looks at the British Labour Government, 1945-1951." *The Historian* 38, no. 1 (1975): 98-100.

Schatz, Arthur W. "The Anglo-American Trade Agreement and Cordell Hull's Search for Peace 1936-1938." *The Journal of American History* 57, no. 1 (June 1970): 86. http://www.jstor.org/stable/1900551?seq=2.

Schenk, Catherine R. *Britain and the Sterling Area: From Devaluation to Convertibility in the 1950s.* London: Routledge, 1994.

Schenk, Catherine R. *The Decline of Sterling: Managing the Retreat of an International*

131

*Currency, 1945-1992.* Cambridge, U.K.: Cambridge University Press, 2010.

Schenk, Catherine R. "The Retirement of Sterling as a Reserve Currency after 1945: Lessons for the US Dollar?" *The World Financial Review*, (May 2009): 511. http://www.worldfinancialreview.com/?p=511.

Sked, Alan and Chris Cook. *Post-War Britain: A Political History.* New York: Barnes & Noble and Sussex: The Harvester Press, 1979.

Skidelsky, Robert. *John Maynard Keynes: Volume Three, Fighting for Freedom, 1937-1946.* New York: Viking Penguin, 2001.

Steil, Benn. *The Battle of Bretton Woods: John Maynard Keynes, Harry Dexter White, and the Making of a New Order.* Princeton, NJ: Princeton University Press, 2013.

"Supplying the Allies: The U.S. Lend-Lease Program." World War II Behind Closed Doors. Public Broadcasting Services. http://www.pbs.org/behindcloseddoors/in-depth/supplying-allies.html.

Thornton, Philip. "Britain Pays Off Final Installment of U.S. Loan – after 61 Years." *The Independent.* December 29, 2006. http://www.independent.co.uk/news/business/news/britain-pays-off-final-instalment-of-us-loan--after-61-years-430118.html.

Toye, Richard. *The Labour Party and the Planned Economy, 1931-1951*, (London: Boydell Press for the Royal Historical Society, 2003), 156.

*Trends in British Politics Since 1945*, Edited by Chris Cook and John Ramsden. New York: St. Martin's Press, 1978.

"The U.K. Exchange control: A Short History," Bank of England, http://www.bankofengland.co.uk/archive/Documents/historicpubs/qb/1967/qb67q3245260.pdf.

Ulff-MØller, Jens. *Hollywood's Film Wars with France: Film-Trade Diplomacy and the Emergence of French Film Quota Policy.* Rochester, NY: University Rochester Press, 2001.

Wevill, Richard. *Britain and America after World War II: Bilateral Relations and the Beginnings of the Cold War.* London and New York: I.B. Tauris, 2012.

Whitham, Charlie. "Seeing the Wood for the Trees: The British Foreign Office and the Anglo-American Trade Agreement of 1938." *Twentieth Century British History* 16, no.1 (2005): 29-51. http://tcbh.oxfordjournals.org/content/16/1/29.full.pdf.

Wiener, Jon. *How We Forgot the Cold War: A Historical Journey Across America.* Berkeley,

CA: University of California Press, 2012.

Wright, Kenneth M. "Dollar Pooling in the Sterling Area, 1939-1952." *The American Economic Review* 44, no. 4 (September 1954): 559-576. http://www.jstor.org/stable/1814109.

Young, John W. *International Relations Since 1945: A Global History.* Oxford: Oxford University Press, 2003.

Young, John W. *Winston Churchill's Last Campaign: Britain and the Cold War 1951-1955.* Oxford: Clarendon Press, 1996.

Zeiler, Thomas W. "GATT Fifty Years Ago: U.S. Trade Policy and Imperial Tariff Preferences." *Business and Economic History* (Winter 1997): 710. http://www.langinnovate.msu.edu/~business/bhcweb/publications/BEHprint/v026n2/p07 09-p0717.pdf.

Printed in Great Britain
by Amazon

33086642R00076